OSPREY
MILITARY • **CAMPAIGN SERIES** 21

GRAVELOTTE-ST-PRIVAT 1870

D1573055

GENERAL EDITOR DAVID G. CHANDLER

OSPREY MILITARY **CAMPAIGN SERIES** 21

GRAVELOTTE-ST-PRIVAT 1870

END OF THE SECOND EMPIRE

PHILIPP ELLIOT-WRIGHT

◀ *Top: St-Privat.
Despite suffering massive
losses on the exposed
slope, the 4th Foot
Guards Regiment
managed to get up and
charge forward to seize
the cemetery. A violent
mêlée ensued as the
French defenders refused
to give ground. (ASKB)*

◀ *Below: Having
reached the northern
extremity of Bazaine's
line above Roncourt, the
Crown Prince of Saxony
directed XII Corps'
assault to clear Pechot's
isolated brigade. Due to
the piecemeal arrival of
XII Corps from its long
march and the dogged
determination of Pechot's
defence, it took almost
two hours to take the
little hamlet. (ASKB)
See page 81.*

▲ *Gravelotte. As night fell the troops of Fransecky's Corps arrived at Gravelotte to find the village crowded with the wounded of* *First Army. Cheered on by many, its 3rd Division was soon added to the toll of fruitless asssaults across the Mance Ravine. Despite a* *long day's march to reach the battlefield, they still managed to advance at the double. (ASKB) See pages 72-3.*

CONTENTS

Introduction	6
The Road to War	7
The Opposing Leaders	11
The Opposing Armies	16
The German Army	16
Organization	17
Armaments and Tactics	20
The French Army	21

The French Army: Organization	25
Equipment and Training	25
Mobilization and Deployment	29
German Mobilization and Deployment	29
French Mobilization and Deployment	32
The Frontier Battles	37
The Battle of Fröschwiller-Wörth	39
The Battle of Spicheren	41
The Retreat to Metz	44
Bazaine Takes Command	46
Moltke Sets the Trap	47
The Trap Closes	49
The Battle of Mars-la-Tour	49
The Battle of Gravelotte-St-Privat	56
The Position	56
Moltke's Plan of Attack	57
The German Advance	61
First Army's Attack	67
The Guard and Saxons at St-Privat	73
Defeat	80
Casualties	86
Judgement	88
Aftermath	90
The Battlefield Today	91
Chronology	92
A Guide to Further Reading	93
Wargaming Gravelotte-St-Privat	94

For a catalogue of all books published by Osprey Military, please write to The Marketing Manager, Consumer Catalogue Dept., Osprey Publishing Ltd., 59 Grosvenor Street, London W1X 9DA

Key to Map Symbols

Army Group	XXXXX ⊠
Army	XXXX ⊠
Corps	XXX ⊠
Division	XX ⊠
Brigade	X ⊠
Regiment	III ⊠
Battalion	II ⊠
Infantry	⊠
Cavalry	◨
Artillery	⊡

First published in 1993 by Osprey Publishing Ltd, 59 Grosvenor Street, London W1X 9DA.

ISBN-1-85532-286-2

Produced by DAG Publications Ltd for Osprey Publishing Ltd. Colour bird's eye view illustrations by Cilla Eurich. Cartography by Micromap. *Wargaming Gravelotte-St-Privat* by Stephen Shann. Wargames consultant Duncan Macfarlane. Originated by DAG Publications in QuarkXPress via TBL, Warley. Mono camerawork by M&E Reproductions, North Fambridge, Essex. Printed and bound in Hong Kong.

INTRODUCTION

The Battle of Gravelotte–St-Privat, fought on Thursday 18 August 1870, marked the conclusion of the opening campaign of the Franco-Prussian War. It had commenced with the fall of Saarbrücken to the French on 2 August 1870, but had ended with the main French field army under Marshal Bazaine blockaded in the fortress city of Metz. The intervening period had seen the apparently invincible armies of Germany's General Moltke sweeping across north-eastern France, inflicting defeat after defeat on the forces of Imperial France. The conclusion drawn by most contemporaries and many subsequent commentators was that it was the inevitable victory of a professionally led conscript army over the amateurism of a traditional long-service army. Further, the campaign established the first claim to military posterity by the German General Staff as being the classic example of strategic planning and organization laying the basis for victory on the battlefield.

Yet the battles from 2 to 18 August all too often give evidence of impetuosity on the part of individual Prussian officers of all ranks, operating with limited reference to central command, and with resultant exposure of their troops, both strategically and tactically. That this weakness was not exploited to any effect by the French was more to do with serious failure in the quality of French command rather than any innate superiority on the part of the German forces. In this respect the Battle of Gravelotte–St-Privat was an appropriate finale to the campaign, exemplifying as it did so much of the fighting of the previous seventeen days. A most un-German lack of restraint by the Prussian General Steinmetz and the less than inspired command of the Guard by Frederick Charles, saw the German forces endure a twelve-hour mauling. As evening fell, more than 20,000 Prussian casualties against

13,000 French lay on the field and a great part of the Prussian king's army was on the verge of retreat. Yet the French command under Bazaine was tamely to lock the intact main French field army up in Metz rather than use its reserve to exploit its enemy's tactical errors. Having safely blockaded Bazaine, Moltke was to finish off the remaining forces of Imperial France two weeks later at the Battle of Sedan, so ending the Second Empire of Napoleon III.

Here it should be noted that although the conflict of 1870-1 is normally termed the Franco-Prussian War, it was actually fought by the North German Confederation formed in 1867 with its south German allies of Bavaria, Württemberg, Hesse and Baden against Imperial France. It is fair to say that a united Germany thereby already existed and its single army fought the war, this despite the fact that the Confederation and its southern allies were not transformed into the Imperial German Empire until 18 January 1871. Hence post 1867, the generic term 'Germany' rather than 'Prussia' or other individual German states forming the Confederation, will be used in the text.

▶ *If any single individual was responsible for the war it was the Chancellor of the North German Confederation, Otto von Bismarck. This archetypal Prussian Junker successfully defeated the German liberals in the early 1860s so as to ensure a Prussian-dominated united Germany. Bismarck's policies were ruthlessly realistic and opportunistic, driven by a vision of the inevitability of German unification. With a view to achieving his ideal he fought three wars: against Denmark in 1864, Austria in 1866 and France in 1870-1. (*Illustrated London News*)*

THE ROAD TO WAR

Few would question the assertion that the Franco-Prussian War was a showdown between an emerging united Germany under Prussia and the — up to this time — senior European power, Napoleonic France. The key player in this struggle was undoubtably Otto von Bismarck.

In 1862 Bismarck had become Minister-President of Prussia, entering office with a determination to unite, under Prussian leadership, the North German State, if not, in time, the whole of Germany excluding Austria. Ever since the events of 1789-1815 the growth of German nationalism had been making continual, if not steady, progress. The French Revolution, Jena-Auerstadt and the War of Liberation had established the bedrock of it.

Despite the reservations of the Prussian and other German princes, the progress had continued to deepen with the Zollverein (customs union) and the Revolution of 1848. As the strongest German state, Prussia was seen as the national focus for unification. In 1859 a conference of democratic German parties at Eisenach set up a national association, the Nationalverein, pledged to supporting the concentration of military and political power in the hands of Prussia. With the appearance of Bismarck on the scene in 1862, a politician capable of exploiting German nationalist sentiment had arrived.

Bismarck did not come to power in 1862 with a master plan for German unification or even a clear vision of what would constitute a united Germany although convinced of its inevitability. Essentially he was a Prussian Junker of genius determined that a unified Germany would be one formed under the Prussian monarchy. Having neutralized the Liberal opposition in Prussia by 1862, Bismarck set about his long-term objectives of a 'Prussian' Imperial Germany by a combination of dexterous expediency, ruthless opportunism and good fortune. The Danish War of 1864 gained Schleswig and prepared the way for the Austro-Prussian War of 1866. The stunning seven-week campaign against Austria saw the total eclipse of Habsburg power in Germany with the destruction of the German Bund created fifty years before by Metternich. It also proved the soundness of the extensive military reforms of Prussia's Minister of War, General Albrecht Roon.

In many ways, the subsequent Treaty of Prague created the basis for a united Germany: Hanover, the Elbe duchies and various smaller states were annexed by Prussia. Further, a new North German Confederation of all German states north of the River Main was established under

▲ *The King of Prussia, William I, might best to described as a passive observer in the events of 1870. While a classic Prussian soldier-king, he was also a courteous man. He had not invited the Spanish offer to his cousin which resulted in* the 'Ems Telegram' and *expressed concern when war was declared. While he accompanied his army in the field, he did little to interfere with Moltke's operational control. (ASKB)*

▲ *In many ways the Emperor Napoleon III was a tragic figure in 1870. A cousin of Napoleon Bonaparte, the first fifteen years of the Second Empire had been a glittering success but by 1870 ill health and poor judgement left his* crumbling regime facing *an almost unstoppable rush to war. His attempt to command his army in the field finally broke him and he was ultimately almost a passive observer of his own downfall. (ASKB)*

Prussian control with Bismarck as its Chancellor. Only the four southern German states of Baden, Württemberg, Saxony and Bavaria retained any real political independence. Yet even they secretly agreed to reorganize their armies on the Prussian model and to ally themselves with the Confederation in the event of war.

The events of 1866 came as both a political and military shock to Imperial France. Under Louis Napoleon, France had re-established her pre-eminence in the European balance of power since 1852. As Napoleon III, he had re-established a stable dictatorship, a working relationship with France's long time-enemy, Britain, and the apparent supremacy of French arms in the Crimean and Franco-Austrian Wars. While Louis Napoleon was no military genius, he certainly possessed great political skill as well as an awareness of military developments and the need to keep pace with them. Yet, while Bismarck's star was in the ascendant in the mid 1860s, Napoleon's was firmly setting. A combination of ill health and growing internal opposition to his rule meant that by 1866-7 Imperial France was limited in her ability to rise to the growing German challenge. The financial scandal and political fiasco of Napoleon's Mexican 'Empire' in 1865 had been followed by his being outmanoeuvred by Bismarck during the Austro-Prussian War. This had seen France remain neutral in the false expectation that she would gain geographically in the western Rhineland. Instead, Napoleon and the French people found themselves facing a resurgent Prussia at the head of the North German Confederation. In France a mood of fear, of anger and even bewilderment began to set in.

Napoleon, the previous glitter and achievements eclipsed, embarked on an ever more desperate series of policies to restore his reign's declining credibility. Meanwhile Bismarck was carefully detaching both Italy and Austria from any possible alliance with France if war should break out. Possibly the only positive action of Napoleon from 1866 to 1870 was a much needed modernization of the French Army in light of Prussia's obvious superiority during the Austro-Prussian War. But, as will be seen, even here Napoleon's declining political power saw sufficient domestic opposition from various parties to leave much military reform still-born at the outbreak of the Franco-Prussian War in August 1870.

It would be fair to say that by 1869 many in both France and Germany expected (and some even desired) war, if only to settle the ever more pregnant question as to who was now the senior European power. While the King of Prussia exhibited little desire for conflict, both Bismarck and the Chief of the General Staff, Moltke, felt a showdown was desirable to cement unification and pre-empt French military reform. Napoleon, like William, demonstrated little enthusiasm for conflict: by 1869-70 he was seriously ill and very aware of French military limitations. Yet the French press, people and politicians of all parties were convinced that France must, and would be, victorious in any war. The trigger came from events which were to be manipulated by Bismarck to cause France fatally to declare war.

Back in September 1868 a military coup in Spain had removed the highly unpopular Queen Isabella II, but this left a vacuum in which no obvious candidate existed to take the Spanish throne. Consequently the Spanish Cortes set out to find a suitable prince, the requirements being that he must be Catholic and not a member of the Spanish Bourbon line. In 1869, after a number of refusals by others, it was offered to the son of Prince Charles Anton of Hohenzollern-Sigmaringen, a cousin of Prussia's King William and the senior member of the Catholic, south German branch of Prussia's royal house. Despite the

family's reluctance to accept, the French government demanded that the offer be withdrawn and Bismarck realized that he had the necessary trigger to cause France to consider war. When, on 19 June 1870, Bismarck persuaded the family to accept the offer, the French Assembly erupted into ferment and demanded action. Despite the misgivings of both Napoleon and the Liberal Prime Minister Emile Olliver, the ardent anti-Prussian Foreign Minister, the Duc de Gramont, dispatched a demand to King William that the candidature be withdrawn and a formal apology offered. The Prussian king received this at Bad Ems where he was taking the waters. William, who had no desire for war to be provoked, received the French Ambassador Benedetti very courteously and made it clear that he had had no role in the affair. As Leopold had withdrawn his offer anyway, the matter seemed settled. William, considering the matter closed, simply refused to discuss it further. He sent a telegram to Bismarck in Berlin outlining the day's events.

Bismarck was at dinner with Moltke and Roon, all three melancholy at the apparent collapse of their provocation to France. The king's prosaic telegram had ended by giving Bismarck authority to publish the factual account. Ever astute given an opportunity, Bismarck seized on the king's authority to publish a carefully edited version which changed not a word. But he altered the emphasis so that it read as though the king had brusquely dismissed Benedetti without a word. The restructured version was published on 13 July as the 'Ems Telegram'.

Paris received it on 14 July, Bastille Day, and the impact was immediate. The press demanded war for the 'insult' and the normal Bastille Day military parade acted as a catalyst — the Paris streets filled with near hysterical crowds demanding war. Senators and deputies of the Assembly alike joined in, and at noon a Cabinet meeting at St-Cloud agreed on a declaration of war. Napoleon tried to dissuade them, but the decision was made. On 15 July, by 267 votes to 10, the Assembly voted the necessary war credits, mobilization having been ordered on 14 July. On the 19th France's declaration of war was

9

dispatched to Berlin, the first communication from Paris to Berlin since 12 July. In the intervening seven days no-one had thought to ask Benedetti what had actually happened at Ems.

Bismarck, Moltke and Roon could be thankful for Gallic impetuosity. It would be a tragedy for France that such purpose and impetuosity was to be absent from the battlefield.

◀ *In many ways the mood of the French press and public was a major factor in the French declaration of war on 19 July. The piecemeal humiliations of the preceding five to six years at the hands of Bismarck and the final insult of the Ems Telegram led to near hysterical demands for war. The recently elected Assembly faithfully reflected the public outcry.* (Illustrated London News*)*

◀ *Although the German public had not been whipped-up to the same degree of fury as the French, when news of France's declaration of war was received the German people felt 'right' was very much on their side. This is reflected in the rapid arrival of the mass of army reservists who answered the posted call-up in the days after 19 July.* (Illustrated London News*)*

THE OPPOSING LEADERS

Neither William nor Napoleon was in any way desirous of this conflict in whose prompting they had played so little part. Neither was to play a crucial role in the subsequent campaign, although they both accompanied their respective armies to war and gave their full backing once war had been declared and accepted. The result of the conflict was to be the Imperial throne of a united Germany for William and tragic exile in Sussex for Napoleon.

William I was the seventh king of Prussia, a stern, courteous, soldier-king. Born in 1797 he had seen a little active service during the War of Liberation against the first Napoleon (1814-15). A Prussian first and foremost, the anti-liberal reactionary views had forced him to seek temporary refuge in England during the 1848 Revolution. He had become Regent in 1858 for his mad elder brother, and succeeded him as king in 1861. While he was at one with Bismarck in the dream of a Germany, united by Prussia, he had disliked the 1866 war with his Habsburg cousins and in 1870 wished only for peace. He also had ample authority to halt Bismarck's machinations yet he did nothing. He was at best naïve in this respect. As it was, the war he did little to create or stop, saw him transformed in January 1871 into Emperor William I of the German Empire, a state that he was to rule until his death in 1888.

Emperor Louis Napoleon III was a nephew of Napoleon I. Born in 1808 to Louis Bonaparte and Hortense Beauharnais, he had been brought up mainly by his mother as they wandered post-1815 through Italy, Bavaria, Switzerland and England. Reared on romantic tales and the reflected glory of his uncle, Louis Napoleon twice made futile attempts to lead Bonapartist risings in 1836 and 1840. Imprisoned after the second attempt, he escaped in 1845 to London where he received a remarkably warm reception as the English

themselves began the process of romanticizing his uncle.

He returned to France in the aftermath of the 1848 Revolution where he demonstrated acute political skill in getting himself elected President of the Second Republic. December 1851 saw a presidential *coup d'état* which a year later was transformed into an Imperial title, and the Second Republic became the Second Empire.

Napoleon was a highly able politician who brought social stability and apparent glory in the Crimean War and the Franco-Austrian War during which latter he personally commanded in the field. While he lacked his uncle's military brilliance, he was not without an awareness of military requirements and demonstrated a keen appreciation of recent technical and tactical developments. After Prussia's triumph in 1866, he in many ways lead the drive against a conservative military hierarchy for radical reform and re-equipment. That these were not fully in place by 1870 was to do with his increasing ill-health. This had affected his political astuteness, with fiascos such as that of the Mexican adventure of 1863-5. Crippled by gallstones, the period 1865 to 1870 saw poor political judgement in foreign affairs, alienating previous allies Austria and Italy, while at home growing opposition to the Empire's authoritarian character forced Napoleon to grant a liberal constitution and, in 1869, elections for a powerful Assembly.

By 1870 he, like William, did not desire the war, yet he did little to prevent the war party driving France to conflict without allies or a plan of campaign. Despite continuous pain, Napoleon attempted to command the whole army in the field, having initially divided it. Possibly his most fateful decision though was to give command of the Army of the Rhine prior to the battle around Metz to Marshal Bazaine who was to snatch

▲ *The almost legendary Chief of the General Staff, Helmuth von Moltke was the architect of Germany's sweeping victory in 1870. His meticulous planning and assertive strategic opportunism secured a classic envelopment of the Army of the Rhine within sixteen days of the opening of the campaign. His failure to exert adequate control of his subordinates in battle is illustrative of his career as a superlative staff officer rather than a field commander.* (Illustrated London News)

The opposing military commanders on the field of Gravelotte–St-Privat could not have been more different. If Moltke was the best example of the Prussian officer corps, Bazaine was the worst of the French. It ought however to be noted that Moltke's role on the field of battle as opposed to strategic planning was limited. Field command on the German side was in the less than capable hands of General Steinmetz and Prince Frederick Charles, the Commanders of the First and Second Armies respectively.

General Helmuth Moltke was one of history's greatest staff officers and unquestionably the architect of victory in both 1866 and 1870. Born of an old Mecklenburg family in 1800, he had moved from the Danish to the Prussian Army in 1821. Having demonstrated at the Kriegsakademie (1823-6) that he was a born staff officer, he gained practical experience in Turkish service during the 1830s. After two decades of staff duty and much impressive writing, he became Chief of the Prussian General Staff in 1857. Moltke demonstrated his sureness in both planning and execution as Chief of Staff of the Austro-Prussian forces in 1864. William rewarded him with full command in 1866 and was himself rewarded by Moltke's stunning six weeks of victory. Similar success occurred four years later in 1870. Essentially Moltke's genius was to apply traditional precepts of strategy to the new mechanisms of execution of the industrial age — rapid mobilization of reserves, surprise concentration of overwhelming strength by the choice of convenient lines of march, and the inspired use of railways for movement and supply. Moltke remained Chief of Staff until 1888, having been created Count and promoted to Field Marshal on the fall of Metz back in October 1870.

While his brilliance utterly outmanoeuvred his French opponents, actual tactical control fell on the less able shoulders of the respective Commanders of the First and Second Armies. The Commander of the First Army was General Karl Steinmetz, one of the oldest serving Prussian officers in the campaign. Born in 1796, he had fought as a lieutenant in the War of Liberation (1813-15). Having won the *Pour le Mérite* in the Prussian-Danish War of 1848, he had dem-

defeat from the jaws of victory at Gravelotte–St-Privat.

Napoleon himself had left the Army of the Rhine prior to the battle on 18 August and was to be dragged along with MacMahon and the Army of Châlons to defeat and capture at Sedan on 1 September. Temporarily imprisoned in Germany, he spent the last two years of his life in exile at Chislehurst in Kent, the Second Empire having collapsed on receiving the news of Sedan.

▲ *General Karl von Steinmetz might best be described as a 'dinosaur'. Having first seen service in the War of Liberation 1813-15, his physical stamina belied his age. His command of First Army was due to his distinction in 1866 as much as to his longevity. He proved to be a* complete liability, *ignoring Moltke's direct orders and blindly committing his troops to suicidal frontal assaults. Moltke was finally freed from his irresponsible conduct when Steinmetz was 'promoted' to the Governorship of Posen. (ASKB)*

▲ *The Commander of Second Army, Prince Frederick Charles, nephew of King William, was an able if somewhat cautious officer. On the morning of the 18th he was to find himself lunging at the unknown quantity represented by the French dispositions. His commitment of the* Guard Corps against St-Privat was *uncharacteristic in its recklessness and was most likely due to an over-strict following of Moltke's morning order to attack the French 'when found'. (ASKB)*

onstrated ability as well as bravery in 1866 with his victory at Nachod which had prepared the way for the main victory at Sadowa. Despite his advanced years, Steinmetz was something of a rebel still, wilful, obstinate and impatient of control — his eagerness to get his forces into action would prevail even if this meant disobeying orders. An indication of his character can be gauged from his wearing — against all existing regulations — of the 1813-15 style, low-crowned peak cap with its oilskin cover. During the opening campaign of 1870 his irresponsible leadership of the First Army nearly upset Moltke's careful strategy (for which Steinmetz had little understanding or time) at Spicheren, and at Gravelotte–St-Privat brought massive casualties and near disaster upon the Army. After Gravelotte he was dismissed to the safety (as far as the Army and Moltke were concerned) of the governorship of Posen. He died in 1877.

The Second Army was commanded by King William's nephew Prince Frederick Charles who had been born in 1828. Brought up and educated as a traditional Prussian prince to be a soldier, he had served in both the 1848 and 1864 wars for Schleswig-Holstein. The Crown Prince was not without military ability, which he demonstrated in the Austrian War of 1866 when he led the First Army with careful, professional competence. While he was nicknamed 'the Red Prince' from the red hussar uniform he normally wore, it gave a misleading impression of dash and vigour. He was a reflective and intelligent officer but over-cautious. His hesitation at key moments in the campaign were to leave elements of the Army dangerously exposed. Despite this, he was promoted to Field Marshal in 1870, and died an honoured soldier in 1885.

For France, command of the Army of the Rhine fell to the popular veteran Marshal François-Achille Bazaine, possibly one of history's most obvious and tragic examples of over-promotion. Bazaine was what might be called a self-made general, for he began military life without any of the advantages of wealth or good birth associated with most Imperial general officers. Just prior to his birth in 1811 his father had abandoned his family without financial support. Having failed the entrance examination to the Ecole Polytechnique, Bazaine enlisted in 1831 as a private in the 37th Infantry. He proved a natural soldier though, and promotion was rapid; he became a sous-lieutenant in the Foreign Legion in 1833. Campaigns in Algeria and Spain saw him demonstrate 'sang-froid' as well as ability and by 1852 he was a colonel with a reputation as one of France's most experienced campaigners. Napoleon's wars brought further promotion and fame: he became a General of Division in the Crimea and was given corps command in the Franco-Austrian War of 1859. Given command of all French forces in Mexico, he successfully unbalanced the country prior to Napoleon's decision to withdraw, which won him his Marshal's baton.

By 1870 Bazaine was France's best known and best loved soldier. But while an excellent corps commander, he was not up to full Army command when the fate of France was placed in his hands by Napoleon on 12 August. The weight of moral responsibility crushed him physically and mentally, and instead of retiring on Châlons via Verdun as ordered by Napoleon, he clung on around Metz, allowing the Army of the Rhine to be cut off. During the battle of Gravelotte–St-Privat he remained far to the rear, hardly intervening in the course of the battle. When tactical victory lay within possible grasp, he did nothing and allowed his right wing to be overwhelmed. He then meekly retired into Metz with more than 175,000 of France's finest troops, surrendering three months later.

After the war he was court-martialled and found guilty of treason. Originally condemned to death, his sentence was commuted to twenty years' imprisonment. He managed to escape in 1874 and lived out his final years in Spanish exile. A tragic figure, this able subordinate commander was over-promoted and simply buckled under the strain of responsibility that his character and intelligence should never have been required to bear.

On 18 August two other French general officers were to play a crucial role. Marshal François Canrobert was France's senior serving Marshal and Commander of VI Corps. An archetypical, dashing beau sabreur of l'Armée d'Afrique, his outstanding record and long experience ought to have made him suitable as a Chief of Staff or even Commander instead of Bazaine. But Canrobert was an ambivalent character who shrank from ultimate responsibility, as illustrated when he had resigned supreme command in the Crimea in 1855. In August 1870, although aware of Bazaine's incompetence for high command, he cynically declined responsibility. As VI Corps Commander he inflicted a murderous defeat on the Prussian Guard at St-Privat which secured his reputation. After 1871 he entered politics as a loyal Bonapartist.

The other key officer was General Charles Bourbaki whose activities on 18 August have been compared to that of a prima donna. Bourbaki was a young general, by French standards, at 54, his rich and well-placed court connections having

▲ *Prior to the events of 1870 Marshal Achille Bazaine was seen as one of France's greatest soldiers. He had risen from the ranks by merit and had won justified renown for his victories in the Crimea, Italy and Mexico. But he had never held the post of Commander-in-Chief prior to 12 August 1870, and he reluctantly* accepted it as the loyal subordinate he always was. His failure was as much the fault of those who 'chose' him as his own inadequacies for such a post. (**Illustrated London News***)*

▲ *Marshal François Canrobert was an undoubtably gifted officer who was reluctant to accept senior command, having turned down the opportunity in the Crimea in 1855 and again on 12 August, preferring instead to remain a corps commander. On 18 August his understrength VI Corps held the* formidable position at St-Privat with his right in the air. Despite St-Privat's intrinsic strength he was denied any support to prevent XII Corps' outflanking movement and his hard-pressed corps collapsed under the sheer weight of numbers brought against it. (ASKB)

done much for his promotion. A graduate of Saint-Cyr, he had demonstrated courage and command ability in Algeria, the Crimea and northern Italy. In 1870 he was commander of the Imperial Guard and highly conscious of both its élite status and its role in the ultimate reserve. It had hardly fired a shot in anger prior to 18 August and as the crisis of the battle developed its commitment might well have produced a French victory, but as it turned out Bourbaki would merely involve his precious guard in the rout of the right wing during the evening and see it locked up in Metz.

Bourbaki himself escaped through the German lines to serve the new Government of National Defence. But the rapidly raised forces he commanded failed to stand up to the seasoned German forces and suffered a series of defeats. His pride broken, he attempted suicide and never again saw active service.

THE OPPOSING ARMIES

The German Army

The Army of the North German Confederation and its south German allies in 1870 demonstrated to the world their superiority throughout the campaign and became the model many subsequently copied. Yet prior to 1862 the Prussian Army from whom they derived their superlative model had been anything but impressive, resting as it had for many years on the laurels of 1813-15.

Its limited conscription for the regular army and almost mythical reliance on the separate civilian Landwehr was still effectively based on the Conscription Law of 1814. This army had been shown to be less than adequate in Prussia's defeat by Denmark in the First Schleswig-Holstein War of 1848-50. Reform, as in France, was to be strongly opposed by both liberal politicians and conservative military officers, but, unlike the situation in France, a combination of determined and talented senior figures successfully pushed through the vital programme of modernization from 1862 to 1867.

The key figure in the reform process was General Albrecht Roon, a loyal yet intelligent supporter of Hohenzollern absolutism who wished to transform the Prussian Army into an engine for Prussian hegemony in Germany. Consequently,

◀ *This idealized view of the troops of the North German Confederation very much reflects the post-1866 reputation they had achieved. While Roon's military reforms ensured that Germany could field more than 1,000,000 men in 1870, in both battlefield formations and armed with the Dreyse rifle, they were, if anything, inferior to the French. This was more than compensated by their sheer 'will to win' and ability to suffer enormous casualties without breaking.* (**Illustrated London News***)*

from 1862 to 1867 Roon, alongside Moltke, saw through a radical programme of reform. This not only remodelled the Prussian Army, but, after 1866, was to transform the army of the North German Confederation.

In 1870 King William of Prussia was Commander-in-Chief of the Federal Army of the North German Confederation. This army was raised by obligatory universal service without substitution. At twenty, a young man served three years in the regular army, followed by four years in the reserve. The 27-year-old then passed to the Landwehr where he remained liable to call-up for another year. A further four years of service, under the direct supervision of the regular army, remained. Hence in 1870 the army could call on all males between the ages of twenty and twenty-eight, thus producing a wartime field army of more than 730,000 men, with almost another 200,000 in the Landwehr as a second line reserve. This vast army considered itself — and drilled the concept into its soldiers — as 'the training school of the entire nation for war', their only loyalties being to King and Fatherland.

The vast expansion of the army meant that the near monopoly of the Junker class of the officer corps was, to an extent, diluted by bourgeois officers, but the new non-aristocrats simply adopted the Junker attitudes and ethos, thereby preserving the social cohesion of the officer corps. In training, Moltke's influence was highly visible, with the stress on personal initiative, flexibility and leadership. While excellent staff officers were produced, in battle many subalterns proved over-eager to push forward. This contributed to the heavy casualties suffered during the early actions of the campaign, up to and including Gravelotte–St-Privat. Ironically, in 1870 strict obedience to orders was not always the German officer's first inclination if the orders inhibited aggressive movement.

Organization

In terms of organization and equipment, the Army of the North German Confederation followed the Prussian model. The army was classified into the corps of the Guards, twelve army corps and one

▲ If any single individual could take credit for the German military machine that was deployed in August 1870 it was General Albrecht von Roon. His programme of military reforms, begun in 1862, transformed an early nineteenth-century 'limited' army into a mass national army of the indutrial age. His concept of true universal service allowed Germany to field more than 1,000,000 men within fourteen days of the declaration of war. (Illustrated London News)

Hessian division, each army corps consisting of two divisions of infantry and one brigade of cavalry, the exception being the cavalry of the Guards and XII Saxon army corps which were consolidated into one division of cavalry. On a war footing this was to consist of 12,777 officers, 543,058 men, 155,896 horse and 1,212 guns (this does not include reserve or Landwehr).

At the head of the army were the three divisions of the Royal Guard corps under Prince Augustus of Württemberg. Its two infantry divisions were each divided into two brigades, each brigade consisting of two regiments. The line consisted of one hundred and eighteen regiments, each of three battalions, two designated as musketeers and one of fusiliers, with the exception

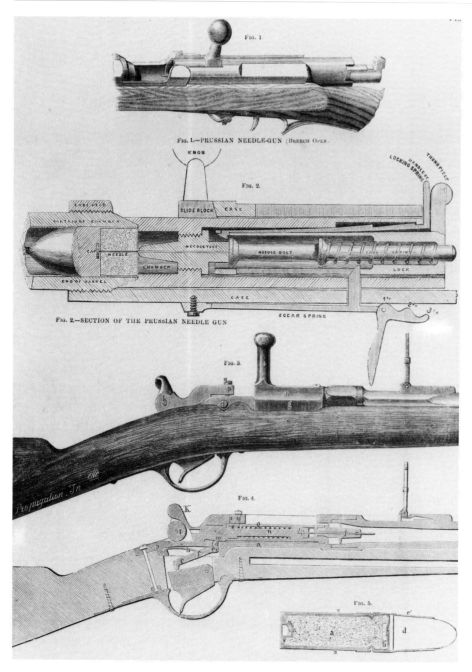

FIG. 1.

FIG. 1.—PRUSSIAN NEEDLE-GUN (BREECH OPEN).

FIG. 2.

FIG. 2.—SECTION OF THE PRUSSIAN NEEDLE GUN

FIG. 3.

FIG. 4.

FIG. 5.

◄ *When introduced in the 1840s and 1850s the Dreyse needle-gun was the most advanced infantry weapon in the world, but by 1870 it had been technologically superseded by the French Chassepot. The Dreyse's exposed firing pin was subject to embrittlement and its machined bolt-action allowed significant escape of gas thereby limiting its range to 600 yards and discouraging careful aim. (ASKB)*

of the four regiments of the Grand Duke of Hesse which had only two battalions each. There were also eighteen battalions of Jäger. Each battalion of infantry numbered 1,000 men divided into four companies. On average line divisions were composed of four infantry regiments divided between two brigades with a cavalry regiment (normally dragoons) attached. Some divisions included a battalion of Jäger. Typical was the 5th Division of General Stülpnagel's III corps which was composed of 9 Brigade under General Döring, including 8th Leib-Grenadier Regiment; 10 Brigade under General Schwerin, including 12th Brandenburg Infantry Regiment; and 3rd Brandenburg Jäger Regiment. The division also included 12th Brandenburg Dragoon Regiment together with two heavy and two light batteries.

The cavalry had seventy-six regiments, including cuirassiers, dragoons, uhlans and hussars. Each regiment had five squadrons of

▶ *Lieutenant and soldier of the 3rd Regiment of Foot Guards, German Guard. Their uniforms differed little from that of the regular line, with the addition of distinctive strips of lace (lutzen) on the collar and cuffs and their own specific helmet plates. Illustration by Les Still.*

which one was a depot squadron, the whole amounting to 700 men. While most of the dragoon regiments were attached to infantry divisions, the balance of cuirassier, uhlan and hussar regiments were in separate cavalry divisions, either attached to the army corps or the general cavalry reserve.

There were thirteen regiments and one (Hessian) division of field-artillery. These were divided at the outbreak of war into field-artillery brigades, each of two regiments. Each regiment generally had three mounted divisions (Abteilungen), each usually of three battalions, and one division of horse-artillery of two battalions each. Each battery contained six guns.

Armaments and Tactics

In terms of armaments, the German Army in 1870 had a mixture of advanced and obsolete weapons. When first introduced in 1848, the Prussian Dreyse needle gun was well ahead of its time, with a range of some six hundred yards and a rate of fire in trained hands of eight rounds per minute. In 1866 it had scythed down the Austrian infantry who were armed with muzzle-loading rifles. The Dreyse had gained near-mythical status overnight, but by 1870 it was comprehensively out-performed by the French 'Chassepot'. The Dreyse had developed little since the 1850s. Its machined metal breech allowed a considerable escape of gas which both limited range and

discouraged a careful aim. The rubber breech seal of the Chassepot overcame both these difficulties. Further, its exposed firing pin was liable to embrittlement and regular breakage in action compared to the Chassepot's enclosed firing pin.

In the realm of artillery it was a very different story. The steel 9cm breech-loading Krupp gun and its percussion detonated shells were a generation ahead of the French bronze muzzle-loaders firing fuzed shells. Introduced in the early 1860s, the Krupp gun had approximately three times the accuracy and twice the rate of fire of the French 4- and 12-pounders. This alone made the Krupp 9cm a formidable weapon, but its effect was enhanced by virtue of its projectile. While the French fuzed shell was limited to certain pre-set ranges, the German percussion shell knew no such limitations. When it struck it exploded.

At Sadowa in 1866 the Krupps were poorly deployed at too great a range over too wide a front with the result that the impact of the breech-loader was less than impressive. By 1870 the lesson had been absorbed and German artillery achieved tactical dominance by massing batteries well within effective range of targets. Again and again, well-entrenched French troops were to be driven from key positions by the weight of accurately delivered explosive shells.

In terms of infantry tactics the German Army was surprisingly oblivious to the firepower revolution it had done so much to bring about. Essentially, at battalion and company level,

◄ *The all-steel Krupps breech-loader was very much the shape of artillery to come. Its rapid rate of fire, its high-explosive percussion shells and its accuracy meant that when properly massed against any given target, it brought destruction within minutes. If it had been used to prepare the way for infantry assaults at St-Privat, the heavy losses suffered by the Guard might well have been avoided. (ASKB)*

▶ *These flamboyant Turcos regiments, derived from France's North African campaigns, epitomize the contemporary popular view of the French Army. Their uniforms were copied by many armies in the 1860s eager to engender the perceived 'glory' of France's military reputation. In practice these regiments operated in the same manner as the standard line regiments during the battle of 1870. (ASKB)*

officers were still trained to lead their men across open, bullet-swept terrain, in close order company columns. The belief was that the speed of such movement would bring weight of numbers to the decisive point. Instead, the opening battles of the campaign, including that at Gravelotte–St-Privat, was to demonstrate vividly the 'bankruptcy' of German infantry tactics. Regiment after regiment aggressively drove forward in serried ranks to be invariably shot down by French infantry dug into defensive positions.

In its turn the 'will to win' of the German officer was to expose the bankruptcy of the French leadership who failed to take any advantage of the tactical potential of the situation.

The French Army

Both to the French and the watching world, the image of the Imperial Army in 1870 was one of martial flamboyance and a long record of apparent victory in the Crimea, Italy and North Africa. Yet the reality behind the image was one of poor organization and a severely limited reserve which

◀ Sous-Lieutenant, 94th Line, and Private, 100th Line.

was to leave it significantly outclassed when matched against the German military machine. Despite reforms in the light of Prussia's overwhelming victory over Austria in 1866, the French Army of 1870 was still very much the long-service, standing army which had been created by Marshal St-Cyr in the years after Waterloo. He had sought to strike a balance between the armies of the First Empire and the *ancien régime*. This had resulted in the 1818 Military Law by which men from each age-group liable for service were chosen by ballot in

officers, 11,347 were ex-rankers and 7,292 graduates from the Academy. This inevitably produced a socially mixed officer corps which lacked the cohesive social homogeneity of the British or Prussian officer corps. Further, as the majority of promoted NCOs had served fifteen to twenty years before promotion, the age range of the Imperial subalterns, captains and field officers was in the forties and fifties. This made for excellent company officers and a close bonding in certain aspects between officers and men. But staff functions, personal initiative and the study of

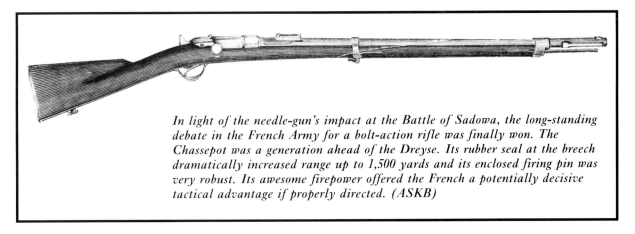

In light of the needle-gun's impact at the Battle of Sadowa, the long-standing debate in the French Army for a bolt-action rifle was finally won. The Chassepot was a generation ahead of the Dreyse. Its rubber seal at the breech dramatically increased range up to 1,500 yards and its enclosed firing pin was very robust. Its awesome firepower offered the French a potentially decisive tactical advantage if properly directed. (ASKB)

sufficient numbers to fill the ranks of the standing army, those chosen then serving for seven years. Yet this system allowed for 'substitution', by which a person chosen by the ballot could pay someone to take his place. Needless to say, the middle and upper classes easily avoided compulsory military service, the ranks being filled almost exclusively by the lower orders.

Meanwhile, the officer corps exhibited a number of serious shortcomings in both structure and ethos. St-Cyr had wished to maintain an avenue of promotion from the ranks and so his Military Law of 1818 had laid down that in order to obtain a commission an individual was required to serve two years as an NCO or pass the examinations at the Military Academy, and that one-third of all new commissions had to go to the ex-rankers. In 1832 this was so modified as to require that the promoted NCOs be from the unit in which the vacancy had occurred. In practice, more than one-third of commissions went to the ex-rankers so that in 1869, of the 18,643 serving

military theory and developments were neglected and despised; officers who studied were openly ridiculed. Added to this, low pay and painfully gradual promotion by superiority provided few incentives for innovation. Finally, because of the significant number of re-enlistments by NCOs after their initial seven years of service, promotion within the NCO corps had become likewise extremely slow, if not ossified, by 1870. Lethargy was all too often the order of the day for officers and NCOs alike.

Having said all this, St-Cyr's army had served the Empire well up to 1866. But the Battle of Sadowa opened a few eyes to its serious limitations with respect to manpower in comparison with the Prussian military machine. After an intense internal debate between the reformers and the traditionalists, the advantage went to the former with the replacement of Marshal Randon by Marshal Niel as Minister of War. Yet the new Military Law passed in January 1868 was still a very poor compromise between the new and the old. While the length of service for a conscript was reduced to five years, with a subsequent four with a newly created reserve, the principle of substitution was preserved. Further, the annual intake was divided into two, the second having to serve only five months. Although a Garde Nationale Mobile was revived requiring all men who had escaped conscription to serve in it for five years, it provided for only fourteen days a year of training and this at only a day at a time. None were spent overnight at a barracks.

It was hoped that by 1875 the regular army would have increased to 800,000 men, with 500,000 in the Garde Mobile, but by 1870 it fell far short of this. When war broke out there were about 250,000 men in the regular army and the Garde Mobile was more of a dream than a reality. The few Garde Mobile units that existed, such as the 18th Parisian Battalion, were hardly more than a rabble. Further, a fundamental tenet of the Imperial Army's philosophy was that the soldier had to be kept strictly apart from the people, in barracks. In this way troops were isolated from potentially seditious influences and fraternization,

◀ *The vast bulk of the fighting fell on the standard line infantry in 1870. Despite poor leadership and an abysmal supply system, they fought with a dogged determination throughout. Ironically their defensive tactics and the superior Chassepot rifle gave them an advantage which was never utilized by inadequate command. Only when exposed to the destructive bombardment of the German artillery did they break, and only then after severe losses.* (Illustrated London News)

but this had a very negative impact in 1870 when sixty-five of one hundred line regiments were not based at their respective depots. Reservists, therefore, had first to travel to the depot to be equipped and then find their parent regiment which by then had often left its garrison for the frontier. Consequently thousands of reservists were to wander in search of their units on an already overloaded rail system and may never have arrived, leaving certain infantry regiments critically below strength.

The French Army: Organization

Organizationally the Army of the Empire was predictably divided between the re-raised Imperial Guard and the line regiments. At Gravelotte–St-Privat, the Guard formed a three-division corps under General Bourbaki. The first division was divided into two brigades of voltigeurs, the second into two of grenadiers. The third Guard division was of cavalry which included the regiments of the Guard Chasseurs, Dragoons, Lancers, Cuirassiers and Carabiniers, each regiment having six squadrons. Each division had two 4-pounder batteries and one of mitrailleuses from the Guard field-artillery. Each battery had six guns.

Each line division normally comprised four line regiments and a chasseur battalion. A limited number of divisions had a zouave or tirailleurs algériens regiment instead of one of the line regiments although none of these were at Gravelotte–St-Privat. Each infantry battalion had eight companies, two each of the 2nd and 3rd battalions forming a 4th depot battalion. An example of a typical line division is that of General Tixier's in Canrobert's VI Corps. First Brigade contained the 9th Battalion of Chasseurs and the 4th and 10th Regiments of the Line. Second Brigade contained the 12th and 100th Regiments of the Line. For artillery support it had two 4-pounder batteries and one mitrailleuse battery attached. Each of the one hundred line regiments had 2,000 men divided into three battalions, each battalion having six field companies and two depot companies. In the confusion of mobilization many regiments averaged only 1,300 men, the ranks often being filled by reservists with a minimum of training.

Each army corps had a division of cavalry attached composed of chasseur and dragoon regiments. At Gravelotte–St-Privat these divisional formations provided the bulk of the cavalry, the only cuirassier regiments being the 7th and 10th in Forton's Division of the reserve. In the army as a whole the fifty line cavalry regiments were divided into ten of cuirassiers, twelve of dragoons, eight of lancers, twelve of chasseurs and eight of hussars. The regiments of cuirassiers and dragoons had four field squadrons and one depot squadron; those of lancers, chasseurs and hussars had one depot and five squadrons. None of the French cavalry formations were to be seriously engaged during the Battle of Gravelotte–St-Privat.

In peacetime, the artillery was organized into fifteen field regiments, four horse regiments and a single regiment of pontonniers. Each regiment had eight field batteries of six guns apiece and four depot batteries. At the outbreak of war these were split up between the infantry and cavalry divisions which had two batteries each. The remaining balance went to each corps' artillery reserve. The mitrailleuses were considered part of the artillery arm but were organized into twenty-four independent batteries. At the outbreak of war each field division received a battery.

The remaining element of the French Army, the regiments of the dashing and colourful l'Armée d'Afrique with its zouaves, tirailleurs algériens (Turcos) and Chasseurs d'Afrique in Du Barail's Division of the cavalry reserve were present at Gravelotte–St-Privat, the 1st and 3rd Regiments having provided Napoleon's escort from Metz to Châlons. The zouaves and tirailleurs were in MacMahon's I Corps of the Army of Alsace (later the Army of Châlons).

Equipment and Training

While the size and nature of the Army had changed little by 1870, thanks largely to Napoleon and Marshal Niel, it was at least armed with an exceptional rifle, the Chassepot. The Battle of Sadowa had vividly demonstrated the inadequacy of the existing muzzle-loaded percussion rifle when matched against the Prussian Dreyse needle-

gun. In fact, an awareness of the need for a new breech-loading weapon dated back as far as 1855 and a few early models had been taken on the 1859 Italian campaign. But the forces of reaction were strong; the Ministry of War feared that the soldier would fire off the ammunition too quickly while the politicians objected to the cost. After Sadowa, however, Napoleon took matters into his own hands. Fortunately, at St Thomas d'Aquin artillery works a M. Chassepot had been working for more than ten years without any official support on an advanced breech-loading rifle. Originally based on the Dreyse, Chassepot had considerably refined and modified the design to produce a virtually new weapon. The most important developments were: first, the insertion of a rubber ring at the breech which significantly reduced the escape of gas, hence significantly increasing its range; secondly, a smaller calibre (11mm) which improved accuracy and reduced overall weight; finally, an improved bolt mechanism which increased the rate of fire.

Sighted at up to 1,600 yards, it outranged the Dreyse by 1,000 yards and its smaller calibre allowed the soldier to carry up to 100 rounds. With Marshal Niel's pushing, nearly one million had been manufactured by 1870.

Another project pushed by Napoleon was the mitrailleuse, an early form of machine-gun. Authorized in July 1866, several hundred were available by 1870. Such great expectations were placed on its battlefield potential that the weapon's existence was kept secret even from senior field officers until the outbreak of war. Developed by an army officer in the early 1860s and partly funded by Napoleon, the concept was to produce the effects of massed infantry or canister fire at 2,500 to 3,000 yards' range. The weapon had twenty-five 13mm concentric barrels operated by a crank handle and was loaded by inserting a block of twenty-five pre-loaded rounds. Ideally, it could fire five 25-round bursts per minute. It was an ingenious weapon, but the intense secrecy which surrounded it (it was

◀ *The French Army felt that it had a decisive 'react-weapon' in the* mitrailleuse, *its twenty-five concentric barrels being capable of five bursts per minute, but the obsessive secrecy surrounding it meant that little thought or practice had been given to its effective deployment prior to the outbreak of war. As it was organizationally attached to the artillery, it was usually deployed too far back to give effective close-fire support to the infantry.* (Illustrated London News*)*

▶ **Grenadier à Pied de la Garde.** *The Emperor's Imperial Guard constituted the epitome of the Second Empire and the Grenadiers stood at its epogee, the direct descendants of the great Napoleon's Guards. In their white-laced blue coats and red baggy trousers, they began the campaign wearing their imposing bearskins but replaced these by the far more utilitarian* **bonnet de police** *by the end of July. On 18 August the Guard were to stand as largely passive observers, denied the decisive role their commander, General Bourbaki desired.*

covered in a tent when fired at demonstrations) ruled out training or useful discussion as to effective deployment. Consequently its twenty-four batteries were deployed as artillery pieces rather than as close infantry support and its potential was never realized.

The weakest aspect of the French Army was its artillery equipment, namely its bronze, rifled, muzzle-loaded 4- and 12-pounder guns. The 4-pounders had been introduced in 1858 at Napoleon's insistence and had done excellent work in Italy. The 12-pounders were older, being rifled ex-smooth-bores, but they fired a usefully heavy projectile for the reserve.

These guns fired three types of projectile: common shell, shrapnel and canister, which were cylindrical in shape and had on the body twelve zinc studs which projected into the six rounded grooves of the canon's rifling. But their effectiveness was restricted by powder fuzes rather than the Prussian percussion fuze. This meant that for the 4-pounders common shells had only two fuze settings: 1,400-1,600 metres and 2,750-2,950 metres, with four for shrapnel at 500, 800, 1,000 and 1,200 metres (those for the 12-pounders were slightly longer). The French shell was capable of ricochet effect and air burst which the German shell was not, but the explosive effect, rate of fire and accuracy of the Krupps more than compensated. Superior German tactical doctrine and training further accentuated this while the French were limited to pre-set ranges.

It was well appreciated that Germany's breech-loaded Krupps were capable of greater range, accuracy and a higher rate of fire than France's muzzle-loaders. Napoleon had attempted to obtain funding for converting to breech-loaders after 1866, but having spent 113,000,000 francs on the Chassepot, the 13,000,000 francs required for the artillery was not available prior to 1870. It ought also to be said that poor deployment at Sadowa had limited the impact of the Prussian guns and so downplayed the potential impact, relative to that of the Dreyse.

Tactically, the infantry was to bear the brunt of the fighting at Gravelotte–St-Privat as it did in the majority of the actions of the campaign, and it did so to the new 1869 drill book. The lessons of Sadowa and the introduction of the Chassepot had caused a lively debate within the army, this being between the traditional school of 'élan' (in effect the shock of the bayonet charge) and those advocating firepower and defensive positions. The 1869 drill was an inevitable compromise, stressing both firepower and élan, but as few officials had had any opportunity to familiarize themselves with it, most acted conservatively and remained on the defensive. Ironically this reliance on the defensive and the long-range firepower of the Chassepot was effective at inflicting heavy casualties on the dense German formations. What was lacking was initiative or leadership to follow up the defensive victories. The moral initiative was invariably surrendered to the Germans.

◀ *Despite long and meticulous planning by the General Staff, the German supply system broke down as the armies moved away from their railheads in the Rhineland. Within days of the opening of the campaign the cavalry was engaged in its traditional role of collecting food and forage from the local population. (***Illustrated London News***)*

MOBILIZATION AND DEPLOYMENT

It might well be assumed that as the French government had taken the initiative in declaring war, it had done so with a clear intention of what its armies would do. In fact, other than a vague objective of meeting the Germans in the field and defeating them, in all the discussions as to whether or not to declare war, the politicians had not considered what they expected the Army actually to do. Given the known fact that Germany could mobilize about one million men against, at best, 300,000 French troops, France's only advantage would be a brief one, that is, in having a standing army rather than a force requiring the calling up of reservists, it could strike first. Instead, while von Moltke's careful pre-war planning successfully mobilized, equipped, and assembled more than one million men within eighteen days of the declaration of war, the French effort was shambolic. Even when assembled the French forces were to lack any clear strategic direction while German forces were to surge forward with carefully planned objectives. As it was, impatience and insubordination on the part of certain senior German commanders was to be the only significant spoke in Moltke's wheel. It was this, rather than any French initiative that presented a number of opportunities for French success; all were to be studiously ignored by the French command.

German Mobilization and Deployment

During the previous eighteen months Moltke and the German Staff had drawn up a detailed plan for an offensive war against France: using detailed maps of eastern France which not only included the smallest road but the number of inhabitants of every town and village, a comprehensive timetable of assembly and invasion was refined. Here the General Staff came into its own for these were professional advisers, not mere adjutants, being selected each year from the outstanding graduates of the Kriegsakademie. Moltke had defined their role as the study of the conduct of war in peacetime and to provide information and advice to commanders in the field during war. They were trained to assess what action was possible within the limits imposed by the technical difficulties of communication and supply. Basically, the General Staff was the Army's nervous system, giving its movements coherence and flexibility. Its specialist transport and logistics officers produced detailed train time-tables that would deliver hundreds of thousands of reservists to regional assembly points. Here they would find their equipment and details of the location of their parent regiment and a ticket for the train that would get them there. During this mobilization phase all rail traffic in Germany was subject to the direction of the General Staff. Further, in the post-mobilization phase, careful planning went into the re-supply of the assembled armies once in motion, although here they under-estimated the ammunition needs and only the relatively low expenditure prevented a crisis. Further, the wagon-trains needed to carry supplies from the railheads to field units proved less than perfectly organized and many supply trains had to search for their units, while they in turn had perforce to live off the land.

In fact, even before war was declared, the Prussian military attaché in Paris had informed the king on 11 July of discreet French preparations for war, and within twenty-four hours German plans were ready for issue. With the French declaration of war, Bismarck immediately invoked the secret clause of the Treaty of Prague requiring the four southern German states to join with the North German Confederation, which they did. Within eighteen

ORDER OF BATTLE
THE GERMAN ARMY

Commander: King William I of Prussia

Chief of Staff: General von Moltke

FIRST ARMY
General Steinmetz

VII Corps
Westphalia: Gen Zastrow
13th Infantry Division
14th Infantry Division

VIII Corps
Rhine Provinces: Gen Goeben
15th Infantry Division
16th Infantry Division
3rd Cavalry Division

I Corps
East Prussia: Gen Manteuffel
1st Infantry Division*
2nd Infantry Division*
1st Cavalry Division

*Infantry Divisions still east of Moselle

SECOND ARMY
Prince Frederick Charles

Guards Corps
Prince Frederick Charles

1st Guard Infantry Division
2nd Guard Infantry Division
Guard Cavalry Division

II Corps
Pomerania: Gen Fransecky
3rd Infantry Division
4th Infantry Division

III Corps
Brandenburg: Gen Alvensleben
5th Infantry Division
6th Infantry Division

IX Corps
Schleswig-Holstein and Hesse:
Gen Manstein
18th Infantry Division
35th Infantry Division
25th (Hessian) Infantry Division

X Corps
Hanover, Oldenburg and Brunswick:
Gen Voigts-Rhetz
19th Infantry Division
20th Infantry Division

XII Corps
Kingdom of Saxony:
Crown Prince of Saxony
23rd Infantry Division
24th Infantry Division
12th Cavalry Division

Reserve Cavalry
5th Cavalry Division
6th Cavalry Division

IV Corps
Detached

Totals: 200,000 men in 210 battalions and 133 squadrons.
First Army: 270 guns; Second Army: 630 guns.
Each division was of two brigades, each brigade of two regiments.
Each infantry division included a dragoon regiment.
Each division had two heavy batteries and two light batteries.

▶ *Trooper, Prussian 4th Uhlan Regiment. The cavalry on both sides played little part in the battle on the 18th, the exception being the ill-fated regiments of the 1st Cavalry Division, directed to charge suicidally across the Mance Ravine. The Uhlans worn the sharply cut* ulanka *tunic and the traditional* czapska *headdress, although the latter was fitted with a black oilskin cover on campaign, with riding breeches and boots replacing leather-lined overalls. Illustration by Les Still.*

*◀ Bavarian jägers. Although apparently still independent, the South German states were bound by secret clauses of the Nikolsburg Treaty to enter the war on the side of the North German Confederation. While retaining their national uniforms, they had, since 1867, re-organized their armies along Prussian lines and easily integrated into Third Army. (***Illustrated London News***)*

days 1,183,000 men had been assembled and 462,000 transported to the French frontier.

Deployed in a wide arc between the Moselle and the Rhine were the Guard Corps, eleven army corps of the Confederation, the Royal Saxon Corps, two Bavarian army corps and a division each of Württemburg and Baden, with 1,194 guns, pioneers, bridging companies, supply, medical services and other auxiliary services, all of which were divided between the three armies. First Army, composed of VII and VIII Confederation Corps, was concentrated around Wadern with the objective of striking through Saarlouis to the Moselle, south of Metz. Second Army, composed of the Guard, III, IV, IX, X and XII Corps, was in the centre, opposite Saarbrücken with the objective of the upper Moselle between Metz and Nancy. Third Army, composed of V and XI Confederation Corps, the two Bavarian corps and the Baden and Württemburg divisions, were concentrated around Landau with the objective of striking through Wissembourg to capture Strasburg. Essentially Moltke's strategic plan was to draw the main French Army forward on to Second Army and then encircle and destroy it, the objective being the conquest and occupation of Alsace-Lorraine.

All that remained was to appoint the senior Army Commanders and it was here that the human factor, the greatest of imponderables, came into play to disrupt Moltke's careful planning. Command of First Army went to the 74-year-old Steinmetz because of his brilliant handling of a corps during the Austro-Prussian War of 1866. Moltke had many misgivings about this obstinate and insubordinate veteran and, over the next two weeks, his fears were to prove well-founded.

Command of both Second and Third Armies went to royal princes, the King's nephew Prince Frederick Charles taking Second Army and the Crown Prince of Prussia, Frederick William, Third Army. Of these two, Frederick Charles proved unpredictable and over-cautious while Frederick William proved both competent and able to follow Moltke's directions. Finally, it ought to be mentioned that Moltke not only had to contend with flawed army commanders, but he and his highly professional Staff found the Royal Heaquarters almost over-run with non-military personnel. There were numerous princes with their courts, a large corps of press correspondents from across Europe, to say nothing of King William and Bismarck's own respective 'assistants'.

French Mobilization and Deployment

Compared to the smooth professionalism of the Germans, French mobilization was grotesquely deficient. The man responsible for mobilization and deployment was General Edmund Leboeuf, Minister of War since the death the previous year of Marshal Niel. While not lacking talent and ability, Leboeuf was unquestionably complacent about France's degree of preparedness. He has gone down in history for his assurance to the Assembly on 14 July, that 'We are ready, very ready, down to the last gaiter button.' In fact, nothing could have been further from the truth. On 14 July the actual order for mobilization was issued, directing reservists to report to their regiments and for regiments to move up to the frontier. Despite several warnings over the previous years from such officers as General Trochu that no planning or preparation had gone into this vital phase, until 8 July almost no thought had been given to the practicalities of this massive movement of men and *matériel* on the French railway network. While thousands of reservists struggled to get to their respective regiments' depots and then move on to join their regiments, the self-same regiments had to leave their garrisons for the concentration areas at the frontier while their supplies had to be dispatched from central magazines to the depot and then on to the regiment. In early July only thirty-six of one hundred regiments of the line were based at their regimental depot. The 86th Regiment of the Line, for example, were in garrison at Lyon, while their depot was in Ajaccio in Corsica.

The chaos of this merry-go-round was further confounded by the intervention of Napoleon. Back in 1868 General Frossard had produced a very competent plan for the deployment of the Army in purely defensive positions on the frontier around Saarbrücken, but the heady days of July in Paris demanded something more dramatic than a defensive posture along the Palatinate. Having spent the period 8 to 11 July preparing corps concentration orders based on Frossard's plan, Napoleon ordered a total reorganization so that he could take personal command of the Army and launch it on an assault of the Rhineland. Part of this optimism was based on the grossly misplaced assumption that the southern German states would remain neutral and that Austria would enter the war on France's side. By the time Napoleon realized that Austria would not enter the war and that the southern German states would (on the side of the Confederation), it was too late to restore Frossard's plan.

The nominal French equivalent of Moltke's General Staff barely rose above a collection of adjutants and clerks selected almost at whim and given no special training. A year before, Marshal Niel had identified the need for qualified and trained officials to be given strategic control of the entire railway network so that reservists, regiments and supplies could be effectively shunted around the system. Nothing in the event was done to effect this, and instead local officials had to book trains in competition with normal civilian traffic and forward these trains to vaguely designated corps concentration areas. The result was that by day 23 of mobilization, 6 August, as the first armed clashes began, only 50 per cent of the reservists had reached their parent regiments and some did not arrive until the battles around Metz and Sedan four weeks later. Many who did reach their units did so without uniforms or equipment. Furthermore, for regiments the question of supplies often became desperate. While ample stocks of equipment, ammunition and food existed, all too often they arrived late or not at all and some formations were forced to requisition bare necessities from the locality. For example in Metz on 28 July there were only thirty-six bakers to provide bread for more than 130,000 troops. Later in the campaign the Germans were to capture vast quantities of French supplies from trains trapped in the clogged rail network.

Despite the complete reorganization ordered by Napoleon on 11 July, the concentration of the Army on the frontier between Luxemburg and Switzerland took place much as had been planned in Frossard's original 1868 plan. This had envisaged the formation of three armies based on Metz, Strasburg and Châlons commanded respectively by Marshals MacMahon, Bazaine and Canrobert; Napoleon's decision of 11 July demanded that there be only one army — the Army of the Rhine — composed of eight corps and lead by the Emperor in person. The three 'dispossessed' Marshals were to be compensated by extra-large corps: MacMahon received I Corps, Bazaine III and Canrobert VI.

Inevitably this juggling created further confusion and produced unbalanced corps as Leboeuf had no option but to improvise. In Alsace, I, V and VII Corps assembled, of which

◀ **Chasseur à Pied,** *9th Battalion. While the specialized arms and role of the* **chasseur** *battalions had disappeared with the general adoption of the breech-loading rifle, their uniforms were distinguished from those of the line regiments. Rather than the greatcoat, in general they continued to wear on campaign their coats with blue pointed cuffs and collar piped in yellow, as were the kepis and blue trousers. The brass buttons bore the battalion number within a buglehorn.*

ORDER OF BATTLE
FRENCH ARMY OF THE RHINE

Commander: Marshal Bazaine

Chief of Staff: General Jarras

Imperial Guard

General Bourbaki

1st Guards Division: Gen Deligny
2nd Guards Division: Gen Picard
Cavalry Division: Gen Desvaux

2nd Corps

General Frossard

1st Division: Gen Verge
2nd Division: Gen Bataille
Gen Lapasset's Brigade
(attached from Failly's 5th Corps)
Cavalry Division: Gen Valabregue

3rd Corps

General Leboeuf

1st Division: Gen Montaudon
2nd Division: Gen Nayral
3rd Division: Gen Metman
4th Division: Gen Aymard
Cavalry Division: Gen Clerambault

4th Corps

General Ladmirault

1st Division: Gen Cissey
2nd Division: Gen Grenier
3rd Division: Gen Lorencez
Cavalry Division: Gen Legrand

6th Corps

General Canrobert

1st Division: Gen Tixier
2nd Division: Gen Bisson
(one regiment strong)
3rd Division: Gen Lafont
4th Division: Gen Levassor-Sorval

Reserve Cavalry

Cavalry Division: Gen Du Barail
(one regiment strong)
Cavalry Division: Gen Forton

Totals: 112,800 men in 183 battalions and 104 squadrons; 520 guns and 150 mitrailleuses.
Unless otherwise indicated each division was of two brigades, each brigade of two regiments.
Each division had two 4pdr and one mitrailleuse battery attached.
Each corps had an artillery reserve of two 8pdr, two 12pdr and two mitrailleuse batteries attached.

the latter two were new formations. West of Alsace, the Guard, II, III and IV Corps assembled, all of which, being pre-existing formations, were tactically fairly well-balanced. Finally there was VI Corps, an entirely new and improvised creation to provide the general reserve, which was gathered at Châlons.

As the formations gathered in late July, the question of what to do with the Army of the Rhine fell largely on the shoulders of Leboeuf as Minister of War. He was acutely aware that Moltke and Roon's military machine could mobilize up to 1,000,000 men by early August

against at best 300,000 French troops and so was conscious that time was of the essence. (In fact, by 28 July, the fourteenth day of mobilization, only 202,448 were recorded as being with the colours.) As he departed Paris for the Army Headquarters at Metz on 24 July, he felt it vital that all eight corps should advance towards the German frontier, regardless of the fact that many units were far from complete, and the corps were strung out over a front of one hundred miles from Luxemburg to Wissembourg. Leboeuf intended that the Army concentrate and thrust into the Palatinate, hoping that the taking of such an

◄ Possibly one of the most able French commanders was Marshal Patrice MacMahon, Duke of Magenta. His distinguished record in the Crimea and Italy ensured high command and despite defeat at Fröschwiller-Wörth and Sedan, few blamed him for the impossible situation in which he found himself. After the war he went on to become the Second President of the Third Republic, having put down the Paris Commune in 1871. (ASKB)

*▼ Saarbrücken. The seizure of this Rhenish town on 2 August was the limit of the much heralded French offensive. After an occupation of less than four days the town was evacuated as the Army of the Rhine began its long retreat. This was not before the French public and press had convinced itself that its seizure proved victory was all but theirs. (*Illustrated London News*)*

initiative would disrupt German troop concentration and draw Austria into the war. But before Leboeuf could initiate his offensive Napoleon arrived at Metz on 28 July, having left the Empress as titular head of a Regency Council in Paris. He immediately countermanded Leboeuf's plans, feeling (with some justice) that the Army of the Rhine was unready for any sort of offensive. Instead, the Army was held in position while Napoleon, subject to increasing indecision and rumour, wondered what to do. Before any decision could be made, on 30 July Moltke made it for him, the Army of the Rhine then numbering 238,188 men against 462,000 available to Moltke.

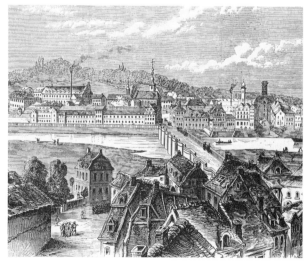

THE FRONTIER BATTLES

As his forces assembled in late July between Karlsruhe and Koblenz, Moltke had finalized his plans for the forthcoming offensive. On his right, Second Army under Prince Frederick Charles was to strike towards Saarbrücken. Its left was to be covered by the much smaller First Army under Steinmetz (134,000 to 50,000) which was to advance in line with it on the Saar. Finally, Third Army under the Crown Prince (125,000 strong) formed the left wing and was to strike into Alsace. The intention was that Third Army would commence its advance in the first days of August, First and Second Armies five or six days later. But delays in the arrival of support units delayed Third Army's date of advance until 8 August. Meanwhile it rapidly became clear that Steinmetz's impatience would pose the greatest threat to Moltke's carefully laid plans, rather than any French potential.

Ironically, while Moltke waited for Third Army to be ready, the French launched their version of an offensive. Lacking any coherent plan, General Frossard's suggestion for the seizure of Saarbrücken was taken up by Napoleon and on 31 July II, III, IV and V Corps staggered ten miles forward. On 2 August six French divisions swept Saarbrücken's two defending infantry regiments out and the French advance came to a 'victorious' halt. This move left the French right over-stretched and the Army of the Rhine inviting a crushing blow against the centre and right by pivoting the German advance on Saarlouis. On 4 August this began. Fifty thousand men of Third Army swept over Douay's division defending Wissembourg, capturing more than 1,000 men but suffering 1,500 casualties itself as the Chassepot demonstrated its effectiveness against the unimaginative German close-order tactics.

After waiting a day for his delayed cavalry to arrive, the Crown Prince continued his march to

▲ *The Commander of Third Army, the Crown Prince of Prussia, Frederick William, was affectionately nick-named 'Our Fritz' by the soldiers. A strong-minded, able and popular commander, he had a distinguished military career dating back to 1866 which he further enhanced in 1870. An opponent of German expansionism, he was married to Queen Victoria's eldest daughter in 1858. He was to die tragically from throat cancer in 1887 having been Kaiser for only three months. (ASKB)*

the north-west towards Haguenau. His innate caution though was already showing as the advance guard of Third Army carefully felt its way forward towards MacMahon's I Corps.

Strategic Situation, 5-6 August 1870

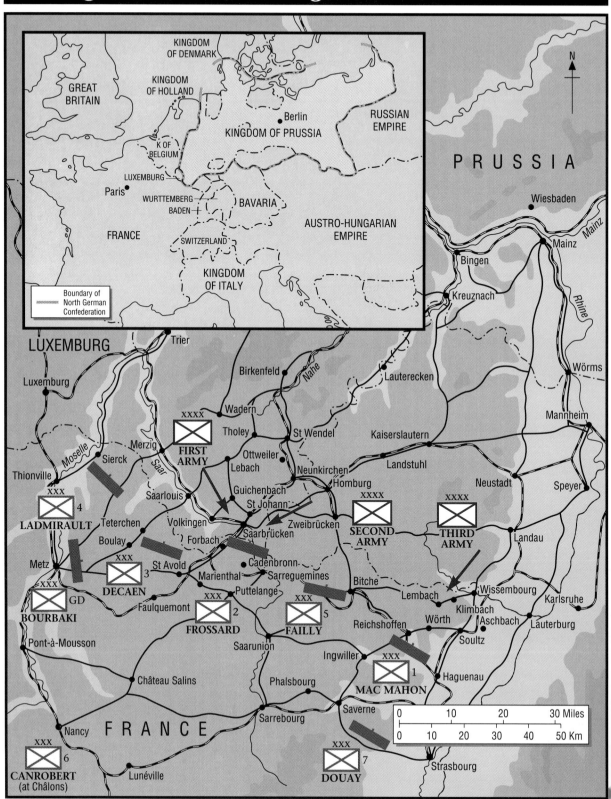

▲General Konstantin von Alvensleben, Commander of III Corps, was to prove an able corps-commander at both Spicheren and Mars-la-Tour. A product of Moltke's General Staff, he had already displayed ability as a field officer in 1866 when he commanded a division with distinction. He combined determination to win with the ability to make cool judgements under pressure. (ASKB)

▲General Edmond Leboeuf succeeded Marshal Niel as Minister for War on the latter's death in 1869 and became Major-General to Napoleon as the campaign opened. He did what he could within the limits of the amateurish French Staff, but with a lack of strategic objectives and inadequate leadership, chaos ensued. When Napoleon departed for Châlons he became Commander of III Corps which performed credibly. (ASKB)

MacMahon was very aware of both his exposed situation and the disparity of numbers (at best five divisions). But Frederick's headquarters at Metz could not countenance retreat or reinforcement of MacMahon with Failly's V Corps (only some fifteen miles to I Corps' left). Instead a not completely unwilling MacMahon deployed the five divisions under his command (three from I Corps, one from VII Corps and one from Douay) from Wissembourg along a wooded ridge above the village of Wörth. These 4,500 men and 100 or so guns then awaited the Crown Prince's Third Army of some 85,000 men and 300 guns. Meanwhile MacMahon dispatched unanswered demands to Failly's V Corps to march to his support.

The Battle of Fröschwiller-Wörth

On the morning of 6 August the German advance guard arrived before Wörth and began a probing attack with 20 Infantry Brigade which was soon joined by the whole of V Corps. In fact the Crown Prince, who had not expected a battle that day and was concerned that his own forces were not yet concentrated, would have preferred to break the attack off until the 7th. But General Kirchbach commanding V Corps' refusal to break off action, and Moltke's clear general order to attack the French whenever contact was made, obliged the Crown Prince to continue the battle. Moreover, two miles to the north of Kirchbach, the commander of II Bavarian Corps, General

Hartmann, marched blindly but loyally towards the sound of the guns. They emerged from the Langensulzbach woods before Ducrot's division whose Chassepot fire brought them to an immediate halt. With the arrival of XI Corps and the Württemberg division on V Corps' left flank, a general assault on MacMahon's position commenced at midday. A fierce battle now developed throughout the afternoon between nine German and five French divisions.

As was to become the very familiar pattern, while the Chassepot cut swathes through the German infantry ranks, the weight of German artillery fire demolished French positions and formations. With more than one hundred guns supporting him, Kirchbach drove across the Sauerbach while XI Corps and the Württembergers moved up on his left and I Bavarian Corps to his right rear.

By early afternoon, though at heavy cost, the Crown Prince had turned MacMahon's right and pierced his centre. By 2.30 p.m. XI Corps had stormed the village of Eberbach while V Corps had taken the shattered remains of Elsasshausen. In a desperate attempt to remedy the situation, the commander of the French right, General Lartigue, ordered Michel's Cuirassier brigade of some 1,000 men, to charge the recently captured village of Morsbronn. The consequence of cavalry advancing on a position defended by two infantry regiments, the 32nd and 80th, armed with breech-loading rifles was inevitable and only a handful escaped destruction.

By mid-afternoon, the final French position on their left, the village of Fröschwiller, fell despite suicidal counter-attacks by two Algerian tirailleur regiments. With no sign of Failly's V Corps which, unlike its German counterparts, was sitting impassively listening to gunfire, MacMahon accepted defeat and ordered a retreat through Reichshoffen. This was covered by MacMahon's only reserve, Douay's weakened division, which temporarily held the centre, and Ducrot's division in the Fröschwiller forest, thereby holding open a line of retreat. Further to delay the Germans another French cavalry formation, General Bonnemain's Cuirassier Division, was sacrificed in a frontal attack towards Niederwald. While three-quarters of it were shot down without a single trooper reaching the German lines, it did delay the German advance sufficiently to allow MacMahon's right and centre to break off action and retreat. But much of Ducrot's division fell into German hands.

The Battle of Fröschwiller-Wörth had cost Third Army more than 10,500 casualties as against fewer than 6,000 French, a testament to the power of the Chassepot. The Crown Prince made no immediate attempt to pursue the French while his battered units reorganized. But

◀ As the Army of the Rhine retreated to Metz, few of the troops had the comfort of tents and cooked food. Administrative chaos left them exposed to the torrential rain that fell from 7 August onwards, and without basic utensils to cook the infrequent deliveries of food. Only when the corps reached the magazine at Metz did the situation improve. (Illustrated London News)

MacMahon's army was almost shattered as it left more than 9,000 men as prisoners of war, together with 28 guns and much of its baggage. His shattered division fell back westward towards Châlons. The Crown Prince's reluctant and improvised battle had won Alsace and opened the road to Paris.

The sweeping, if not fully expected victory at Fröschwiller-Wörth fitted in well with Moltke's strategic plan. He now intended that Second and First Armies hold the main French forces before Saarbrücken while Third Army swung north to roll them up. But now Steinmetz intervened to disrupt this.

While Third Army had been advancing into Alsace, Moltke had concentrated Second Army north of the Saar in order to receive the expected French attack. On 3 August Moltke ordered Steinmetz to concentrate First Army around Tholey to cover Second Army's left flank. But Steinmetz had different ideas. He replied to Moltke by unilaterally assuming the offensive towards Saarbrücken. Not only was this rank insubordination, but it meant that First Army would cut directly across the main axis of Moltke's carefully detailed march-tables and routes. Deaf to Moltke's immediate protests, Steinmetz commenced his advance on 5 August, thus committing Moltke to an offensive by First and Second Armies whether he wished it or not.

As it was, the French advance on Saarbrücken on 2 August had in fact exhausted their offensive initiative. It is doubtful whether Napoleon and Leboeuf would have obliged Moltke by moving the Army of the Rhine forward — since 2 August the irresolution and lack of purpose at the Imperial headquarters in Metz was reflected by the various corps of the Army of the Rhine which was marched back and forth. The intention had been to continue a limited advance with Ladmirault's IV Corps up the Saar valley but as reports came in of First Army's advance and the German victory at Wissembourg, innate caution reasserted itself. Ladmirault was ordered to fall back behind Saarbrücken, but he argued that this would expose the Moselle valley so Napoleon allowed Ladmirault to concentrate farther to the north, moving Bazaine's III Corps to cover the gap. The consequence of thus indulging his corps commanders was that Frossard's II Corps was left dangerously isolated. On 5 August Frossard consequently fell back two miles from Saarbrücken to the very strong position around Spicheren and Forbach, hence by the morning of the 6th the French gains of 2 August had vaporized and II Corps was to find itself in the path of the German advance initiated by Steinmetz.

The Battle of Spicheren

Frossard's 22,800 men occupied a 'position magnifique', the centre being the heights of the towering ironstone cliffs of the Rotherberg. To the right was a densely wooded slope and on the left a narrow valley down which ran the Saarbrücken–Forsbach road. As an engineer officer Frossard appreciated the role of entrenchment and this already strong position was enhanced with the spade by the morning of the 6th. Despite its innate strength as a defensive position, all three of Frossard's divisions were fully deployed to cover its length. If subjected to a major assault, he would rely on the arrival of other corps to hold it.

On the morning of 6 August General Kameke's 14th Division of First Army's VII Corps arrived before Spicheren and immediately prepared an assault. Behind him the overlapping First and Second Armies were moving through and around Saarbrücken. Behind Frossard, on an arc some fifteen miles long, lay the four divisions of Bazaine's III Corps. Basically some 55,000 French troops could reach Spicheren that day against only some 43,000 Germans. With Kameke about to lead a bull-headed assault against Frossard's entire corps, the scene looked set for an easy French victory. The very opposite was to occur.

At noon Kameke launched his division in an assault across the open ground before the Spicheren heights (his corps commander, the ancient Zastrow, did nothing to restrain him). Thanks to the use of open formation and poor French artillery support, 14th Division managed to gain the foot of the Rotherberg and a series of heroic, if desperate, assaults headed by the 74th Regiment up the cliffs and crevices secured a foothold on the summit. Yet Frossard made no significant effort to dislodge these few isolated companies of the 74th and 40th Regiments, being satisfied apparently simply to contain them. Meanwhile, all German formations within earshot were marching towards the sound of the guns; Bazaine's division remained where they were as mere spectators.

By 3 p.m. German troops were arriving together with significant numbers of guns. General Alvensleben now assumed overall command of the arriving German formations and the soon to be familiar pattern began to emerge. While the Chassepot held the German infantry in check, the German artillery was soon pounding the French positions. From 5 until 7 p.m. the bulk of First Army's infantry and Alvensleben's III Corps of Second Army launched a series of fierce assaults on Frossard's positions. On the wooded French right the fighting swayed back and forth through the Giferts Forest at the foot of the Rotherberg. Despite a marked inferiority in numbers, localized French counter-attacks by Laveaucoupet and part of Bataille's divisions with the aid of the Chassepot, twice repulsed the assaults by Alvensleben. By 7 p.m. some thirty German infantry companies were halted in a confused mass in the Giferts Forest. On the French left, Verge's division, supported by part of Bataille's division, repulsed every German assault down the Forbach road on the village of Stiring-Wendell.

By 7 p.m., despite a magnificent defensive action, Frossard was forced to retire. There was no sign of the assistance he had repeatedly requested from Bazaine and his left flank was being progressively turned by General Glumers' 13th Division. Covered by a massed battery of 58 guns before Spicheren, Frossard's troops slipped away in the darkness. Essentially it had been a repeat of Fröschwiller-Wörth: while German commanders had marched instinctively towards the sound of the guns without need of prompting, French commanders had remained inert within sight of the battlefield.

By the end of the day, many German formations were left shaken and disorganized, having suffered more than 5,000 casualties against Frossard's 2,000. Yet the French had left almost 2,000 unwounded prisoners in German hands and had wasted a potential opportunity to inflict a significant rebuff on Steinmetz. At this stage many French soldiers, officers and men alike, were asking themselves if their personal bravery was being sacrificed by inept and irresolute leadership as a general retreat began.

◄ *During the retreat to Metz the German cavalry easily outclassed its French counterparts. Not only were they able to maintain contact with the retreating French corps, thereby providing Moltke with valuable intelligence, but were also to send patrols deep behind French lines spreading confusion and uncertainty in their wake. (*Illustrated London News*)*

Battle of Fröschwiller-Wörth, 6 August 1870: situation at noon

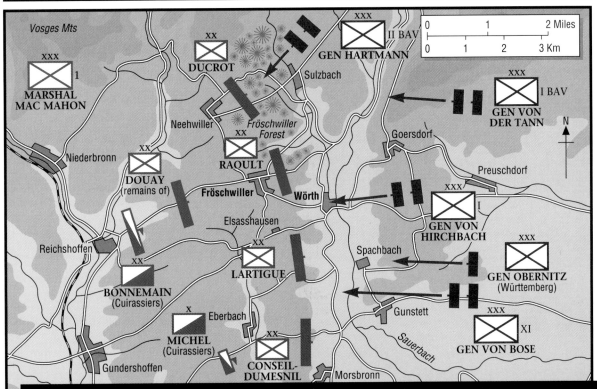

Vosges Mts

MARSHAL
MAC MAHON

DUCROT

GEN HARTMANN

II BAV

Sulzbach

I BAV

GEN VON
DER TANN

N

Neehwiller

Fröschwiller
Forest

Goersdorf

Preuschdorf

Niederbronn

DOUAY
(remains of)

RAOULT

Fröschwiller

Wörth

GEN VON
HIRCHBACH

I

Reichshoffen

Elsasshausen

Spachbach

GEN OBERNITZ
(Württemberg)

BONNEMAIN
(Cuirassiers)

LARTIGUE

Gunstett

GEN VON BOSE

XI

MICHEL
(Cuirassiers)

Eberbach

Sauerbach

Gundershoffen

CONSEIL-
DUMESNIL

Morsbronn

Battle of Spicheren, 6 August 1870: situation at 5 p.m.

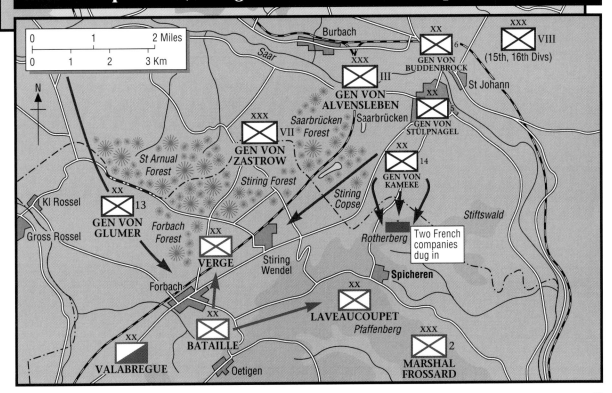

Burbach

GEN VON
BUDDENBROCK

VIII
(15th, 16th Divs)

Saar

III

GEN VON
ALVENSLEBEN

St Johann

GEN VON
STÜLPNAGEL

N

Saarbrücken
Forest

Saarbrücken

VII

GEN VON
ZASTROW

St Arnual
Forest

Stiring Forest

GEN VON
KAMEKE

14

Stiftswald

KI Rossel

Stiring
Copse

GEN VON
GLUMER

13

Forbach
Forest

Rotherberg

Two French
companies
dug in

Gross Rossel

VERGE

Stiring
Wendel

Spicheren

Forbach

LAVEAUCOUPET

VALABREGUE

BATAILLE

Pfaffenberg

MARSHAL
FROSSARD

2

Oetigen

43

THE RETREAT TO METZ

The dual defeats at Fröschwiller-Wörth and Spicheren on 6 August brought about a radical reassessment of the situation by French headquarters and the government back in Paris. Any remaining hope that Austria or Italy would enter the war on their side evaporated, and in Paris the initial euphoria vanished. The government of Olliver, now seen as weak and unprepared, was brought down and he was replaced as Premier on 9 August by General Count Palikao. He was perceived as being a tougher and more appropriate leader in the situation now confronting France. Palikao immediately announced the formation of two new army corps, XII and XIII, together with the calling up of 450,000 barely trained reservists. Yet all these measures would take weeks if not months to execute and the Imperial forces did not have the luxury of time.

The defeats at Fröschwiller-Wörth and Spicheren were in no sense militarily decisive and thanks to Steinmetz Moltke was having to extemporize a whole new strategic plan. But on the morning of 7 August Napoleon's resolution collapsed. He issued orders for the entire army to fall back upon Châlons-sur-Marne, thereby handing Moltke the strategic initiative. Having said this, it made sound strategic sense to fall back and concentrate all available troops between Moltke and Paris. Unfortunately for Napoleon, MacMahon, in the aftermath of Fröschwiller-Wörth, was retreating south-west through the Vosges, thereby increasing the gap with the main body of the Army of the Rhine. Further, Frossard, upon hearing of MacMahon's defeat independently decided to fall back towards Metz without informing Napoleon. When Napoleon was informed of these moves late on the 7th he felt obliged to alter the point of concentration to Metz for the Army of the Rhine while MacMahon and Failly's Corps continued on to Châlons to become the Army of Châlons under MacMahon's overall command. Once concentrated at Metz, the Army of the Rhine would retreat via Verdun to Châlons to secure the original intention.

As a point at which to bring the Army of the

◀ *While the burden of command mentally oppressed Napoleon, his physical presence was undoubtably welcomed by his Guard who felt a close bond to their Emperor. Having handed over command to Bazaine on 12 August, he did not actually depart Metz until the morning of the 16th, spending his time visiting various corps and inidividuals in a 'long goodbye'.* (**Illustrated London News***)*

Rhine together, Metz had much to recommend it. The city was encircled by powerful forts, it contained vast quantities of stores and on 7 August it was still connected by rail to Châlons, although this was to be cut within two days by German cavalry patrols. What was overlooked, however, was that Metz would present a potential bottle-neck unless great care were taken to stagger the arrival of the various corps. Any delay at Metz would permit the Germans to close the gap or even envelop the French with their superior numbers. This is very much what transpired.

While the various French corps were falling back, the pre-6 August confusion repeated itself. As an incessant downpour replaced the previous clear weather the troops had to trudge along muddy roads to water-logged camps. With no real thought being given to march routes, corps and baggage trains soon became entangled and many soldiers subsequently went hungry. Even when food arrived, the rain and a lack of cooking utensils, many having been thrown away or lost after the early battles, prevented the soldiers preparing it. Needless to say, discipline was soon lost and French villages were quickly stripped of food, wood and bedding by the troops.

Yet on 7 August Moltke was having his own difficulties. As a result of Steinmetz's impetuosity and disobedience First Army and part of Second were now entangled in and around Saarbrücken. He had to sort out the confused mass of soldiery and re-impose some degree of strategic control. Moltke issued orders for First Army to revert to its original role of masking the left flank of the French Army while moving out of the way of the much larger German Second Army which could then resume its advance south-west. Needless to say, Steinmetz ignored these directions which would consign him to a secondary role and simply cut his communications with Royal headquarters and allowed the confusion at Saarbrücken to continue. The prolonged delay allowed Ladmirault's IV Corps, lying exposed on the French left, to break contact and join the general movement on Metz.

Once the tangle at Saarbrücken had been sorted out the same confusion threatened to repeat itself in the rain-soaked French lanes. It is a testament to both the discipline and organizational qualities of the German Army that the confused mass of vehicles and men was sorted out and the pace of the advance resumed within three days. Meanwhile, being particularly ill-served by his cavalry reconnaissance, it was not until the 9th that Moltke felt he had sufficient information to issue detailed orders for the pursuit.

Once confident that the two wings of the French Army were marching away from each other, Third Army was detailed to continue in pursuit of MacMahon. First and Second Armies were directed to concentrate towards Metz where Moltke now correctly predicted a decisive action could be brought about.

By 9 August, despite rain and administrative chaos, the four corps of the French left were safely behind the River Nied. They were now joined by the bulk of Marshal Canrobert's VI Corps which had been brought by rail from Châlons to Metz, but in the confusion much of the corps artillery and baggage had been left behind, a deficiency which was to have serious consequences at St-Privat nine days later.

Now Napoleon sought to remove the burden of sole command from his own shoulders. With Leboeuf's support he gave Bazaine command over II, III and IV Corps, General Decaen replacing Bazaine in command of III Corps. But even as Bazaine's new command tried to settle down the poverty of French cavalry in their role of screening the position was displayed. A handful of German cavalry patrols was able to subject the French to constant false alarms and interruptions.

Meanwhile Leboeuf had been trying to summon MacMahon and Failly to entrain their troops for Metz rather than Châlons. Neither took any notice and on 10 August their forces entrained at Lunéville for Châlons. Without these troops and with alarming messages emanating from Paris about a phantom German army of 500,000 massing on the Luxemburg border, the Nied line was adjudged unsustainable. On 11 August the west bank of the Nied was abandoned and Bazaine fell back under the guns of Metz to the east bank of the Moselle.

Finding the Nied clear of French troops, Moltke ordered a halt of two days to allow the ten

Strategic Situation 14-15 August 1870: Moltke swings south

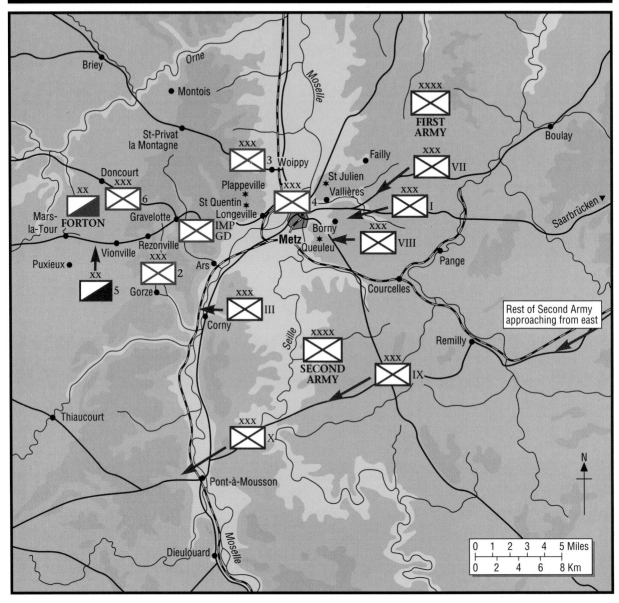

corps of Steinmetz and Frederick Charles to concentrate between Boulay and Faulquemont. With more than 200,000 men concentrated, the German advance resumed on 12 August towards some 180,000 French troops now crowding in upon Metz.

Bazaine Takes Command

On 12 August Napoleon decided to hand over command in order to relieve himself of the ever

greater mental burden oppressing him at Metz, as well as to restore confidence in the army command. Bombarded by negative political news and the growing evidence of military unpreparedness, he felt it best to focus on restoring the political situation in Paris. The key question was: to whom should the military command at Metz pass?

There were nominally four serving Marshals of France from which to choose: MacMahon, Leboeuf, Canrobert and Bazaine. MacMahon was geographically absent, while Leboeuf was discredited by the mismanagement of the campaign, having been forced by Paris to resign as Minister of War on 9 August. Canrobert was the most qualified, but at Sevastopol fifteen years before, he had demurred from taking such responsibility. Further, back in Paris, Palikao needed the support of the radical left and Canrobert's high profile involvement in Napoleon's original coup d'état in 1851 politically ruled him out. This left Bazaine.

Bazaine was politically acceptable to the left because of his ex-ranker background and general lack of political ties. His long record of courage on the field of battle made him a popular choice for the press and public. Militarily his successful record in North Africa, the Crimea, Italy and Mexico bid fair to restore the soldiers' confidence in their command. But his sulky and cautious conduct of the campaign so far ought to have sounded warning bells as to his limitations as a commander-in-chief. As it was, there was no obvious alternative, he was generally a popular choice and Napoleon wanted to relieve himself of the burden. Like a good soldier Bazaine accepted his appointment without complaint or enthusiasm.

Napoleon now prepared to depart for Châlons, although he was to linger at Metz until the 16th, thereby effectively undermining Bazaine's authority and almost non-existent confidence. Bazaine was none the less left with little guidance other than the assumption that he was to defend France from the Germans. Napoleon had not offered and Bazaine had not asked for details of the enemy's movements, about supplies, reserves, or even the general French military situation. It was not until late on 13 August that Napoleon deigned to inform Bazaine that he was to fall back from Metz to Châlons via Verdun, hence it was not until the 14th that this movement began. Finally, Bazaine was forced to accept Leboeuf's assistant, General Jarras, as his Chief of Staff, an officer he neither liked nor trusted. Consequently Bazaine ignored him and sent his orders direct to his subordinates. Movement and supply soon fell into even deeper confusion and Bazaine's obvious lack of enthusiasm and confidence soon transmitted itself throughout the army.

Moltke Sets the Trap

While the matter of the French command was being sorted out, Moltke initiated his strategic envelopment of the French forces at Metz. First, Second and Third Armies were now to advance on a broad front of some fifty miles, sweeping to the south of Metz and its powerful forts. The objective was irrevocably to divide Bazaine and MacMahon, then all three armies were to swing north behind Metz. MacMahon at Châlons was to be ignored until the French forces around Metz were destroyed or contained.

As was now all too familiar, Steinmetz soon forced a modification of the plan's execution, although now with defiant timidity rather than impetuosity. While Second Army swept towards the Moselle on the 13th, First Army crept forward making no attempt to bypass Metz to the south as ordered. While Third Army had boldly raced forward as ordered, the Germans were advancing, not on a broad line but in 'oblique order', Frederican tactics on the strategic level. Rather than try to restore his original intention, Moltke adjusted his strategic plan, turning Steinmetz's disobedience to his advantage.

When ordering his armies forward on the 12th, Moltke had assumed that the French had already crossed to the west bank of the Moselle. When, on the 13th, he discovered that they were still on the east bank, Steinmetz was ordered to halt his already slow advance in order to hold the attention of the French. Meanwhile Second and Third Armies were hurried on their swing north to fall on the flank and rear of Metz. Second Army now became the hub of a wheel while Third Army was the rim and hence moved the quickest. Two corps were temporarily detached to Steinmetz from Second Army in case the French turned on him.

Any fear that Steinmetz might be subject to attack was dispelled on the morning of the 14th when cavalry patrols reported the French as having moved back across the Moselle. Having replaced four pontoon bridges previously washed away, the French corps were queuing to cross the Moselle on a front of less than three miles. Displaying the familiar administrative confusion,

◄ Having bid farewell to Bazaine, Napoleon departed along the Verdun road just prior to its closure by the advancing Germans. He took as his escort the 1st and 3rd Regiments of **Chasseurs d'Afrique,** *an advisable move given the proximity of Redern's cavalry. (ASKB)*

the troops leisurely crossed the pontoon and permanent bridges to march through the narrow streets of Metz. Without clearly identified march routes the various columns soon criss-crossed and jammed the roads.

Having crossed the Moselle, the French corps were to take one of two routes to the Verdun road. The first route climbed direct to the Gravelotte plateau and then through the villages of Rezonville, Vionville and Mars-la-Tour towards Verdun. The second moved around the forts of Plappeville and St-Quentin then north by the villages of Woippy and St-Privat.

Due to the confusion and delay of the crossing, by the morning of the 15th only the Imperial Guard, VI and II Corps were in position on the west bank around Rezonville and Gravelotte respectively. Meanwhile Second Army's 5th Cavalry Division under General Rheinbaben had already crossed the Moselle fifteen miles to the south at Pont-à-Mousson the day before. Further the cavalry of Third Army had occupied Nancy and its river crossing thirty miles to the south of Metz. Given that it was now obvious that Metz was being rapidly outflanked and that MacMahon was not going to be able to reach Metz, falling back towards Verdun quickly was vital for Bazaine. Yet already on the 15th, Rheinbaben's 5th Cavalry Division had moved twenty-five miles north. Its advanced brigade

under General Redern had made tentative contact with the French cavalry outposts of Forton's division at Vionville on the Verdun road. Although isolated for the time being, Redern's troopers were already poised on the French line of retreat while half of Bazaine's army had yet to cross the Moselle.

Meanwhile, on the 14th, one of Steinmetz's subordinates, General der Goltz commanding 26 Infantry Brigade, had initiated yet another pointless assault. Arriving on the rising ground above the Moselle he had found Decaen's four divisions of III Corps still on the east bank. He immediately attacked, drawing in more than five German divisions by evening to no great effect. The Battle of Borny cost the Germans 4,620 casualties against 3,915 French and achieved little beyond delaying the retreat of III Corps. Steinmetz had spent the day sitting impassively as an observer to this pointless action and Moltke now issued the strictest orders to him that First Army was not to become involved in any further action unless specifically ordered. Finally, as regards the Battle of Borny, given Bazaine's performance over the next four days, it should be noted that when Decaen was killed, Bazaine had taken personal command. He had dashed about the battlefield to good effect even when slightly wounded by shrapnel in the shoulder. Unfortunately this seems to have ended his dynamism.

The Trap Closes

The Battle of Borny had delayed Bazaine's final order for the general retreat on Verdun until 10 a.m. on the 15th, by which time German patrols were already astride the road to Verdun with their infantry only a day's march behind. II and VI Corps took the southern route via Vionville and Mars-la-Tour, while the IV and III Corps went via the more northern Doncourt road with the Guard following. Leboeuf, no longer Minister of War or Chief of Staff, took command of III Corps in consequence of Decaen's death at Borny. Laveaucoupet's division, weakened at Spicheren, was to remain to garrison Metz.

The single road from Metz to Gravelotte was soon swamped with thousands of military vehicles to which were now added thousands of fleeing civilians. Even when the columns split at Gravelotte along the Vionville and Doncourt roads respectively, progress was still painfully slow. By the evening of the 15th, II Corps had only reached Rezonville and VI Corps had not even reached Doncourt. Furthermore, the two cavalry divisions, Forton's and Barail's, which were providing scouts and cover to the flanks, were north of the Vionville road. When, on the morning of the 15th, Forton made contact with Redern's scouts, he made no significant effort to ascertain the general situation. When Bazaine was informed of the contact he simply acknowledged the information without further inquiry.

On the morning of the 16th Napoleon finally took his leave of Bazaine. With the 1st and 3rd Regiments of *Chasseurs d'Afrique* to escort him through German cavalry patrols to Verdun and accompanied by his son, Napoleon's final words were to urge Bazaine to hurry the retreat to Verdun. Then, as the sun rose, Napoleon bid goodbye at the Gravelotte crossroads. Later in the day he would hear the gunfire of battle as Moltke closed off the avenue of retreat Napoleon had just travelled. When he arrived at Verdun he took train for Châlons and MacMahon.

Back at Gravelotte, Bazaine received further news of sporadic contact with German cavalry patrols to the west and south of Vionville. Consequently he decided to halt II and VI Corps to await events. This was possibly the fatal decision of the campaign because with every passing second the avenue of retreat was being progressively closed, for to the south Moltke was busy, having temporarily halted Second Army on the Moselle in case Steinmetz was attacked on the morning of the 15th. Once Redern had reported the long straggling French columns crawling west out of Metz, Moltke seized the opportunity. Second Army was hurried on north from its crossing point at Corny to be followed by First Army.

Yet again, however, Moltke's careful strategic conception was almost fatally compromised by his immediate subordinate. Frederick Charles unilaterally decided that his army should move due west not north. He assumed wrongly that by the morning of the 16th the French would be well on their way through Mars-la-Tour. He was not to know that Bazaine had halted his entire army the previous evening to await events! Consequently only III and IX Corps moved north-west towards the Vionville road with X Corps slightly to the west towards Fresnes. Meanwhile IV, XII and Guard Corps marched west away from the French while only First Army's VIII Corps had crossed the Moselle(at Corny) by the morning of the 16th. VII Corps was in the process of crossing while I Corps was still on the east bank at Courcelles-sur-Nied.

The Battle of Mars-la-Tour

On the morning of the 16th the bulk of the French Army was spread in an almost static arc from Forton's cavalry at Vionville in the south to III Corps at Vernéville in the north. Bazaine's postponement of the march that morning had left II and VI Corps relaxing at Rezonville with the Guard at Gravelotte, while IV Corps was still struggling to free itself from the narrow streets of Metz.

At about 9 a.m. German artillery shells fell upon Forton's division encamped at Vionville as the advanced guard of Alvensleben's III Corps arrived. Forton was able to drive the advance guard back on to the body of III Corps which now assembled on the heights just south of

▲ *The 61-year-old General Voigts-Rhetz was Commander of X Corps, yet despite hard living in the field he was to retain the physical activity of a much younger man. At the*

Battle of Mars-la-Tour he was able to support Alvensleben in that desperate battle and was to serve credibly throughout the remainder of the campaign. (ASKB)

Rezonville. Alvensleben was not one to shirk battle and, believing that he was dealing with the French rearguard, divided to attack in an attempt to cut off its retreat. He was convinced, as was Frederick Charles, that the main body of French troops was already well to the west on the way to Verdun. In fact, the shells which alerted Forton's bivouacs meant that III Corps was advancing against three deployed French corps, III, VI and Guards. As Alvensleben's infantry emerged from Gorze on to the open plateau, they were confronted by Frossard's II Corps deployed from Vionville through Rezonville to the ravine of the Juree stream. Behind II Corps was VI Corps

drawn up just north of Rezonville with the Guard to the east at Gravelotte. Undeterred, the forceful Alvensleben launched General Stülpnagel's 5th Division forward to see it suffer heavily. But it fixed Frossard, and Bazaine did nothing to move VI Corps or the Guard to counter-attack. Stülpnagel was completely repulsed but meanwhile fifteen German batteries of artillery had been established on the heights south-west of Flavigny which dominated the whole French position.

Alvensleben now realized that he was facing the entire French Army rather than its rearguard and that to survive he had to convince the French that they faced the entire German Army, not just a corps. His 6th Division, which had been advancing upon Mars-la-Tour (already held by Rheinbaben's cavalry), was swung eastwards to attack Vionville. This quickly fell, there being only a single regiment of chasseurs to defend it. Supported by the massed batteries to the south-west, 6th Division pushed into Flavigny but were then halted. From then on, more and more guns were to be massed in an arc from Mars-la-Tour to the Bois de St-Arnould until by evening 210 guns were engaged. They were to provide the vital support to the desperately outnumbered infantry as the day wore on.

On the face of it, Alvensleben was in a serious situation with both divisions committed, X Corps still marching towards the sound of the guns while before them II and VI Corps' lines were being strengthened by the arrival of the III Corps from Vernéville to the north-east. But Bazaine was not the commander to seize the opportunity to destroy III Corps. All he could see was a threat to his left flank and his communications back in Metz, so he concentrated the Guard, II Corps and parts of VI and III Corps around Rezonville to secure his left and the road back to Metz. Meanwhile Frossard, with his right turned at Vionville, considered his situation desperate and called for cavalry support to secure his open right. Despite protests from their colonels, Frossard launched the Cuirassiers and Lancers of the Guard against the unbroken lines of German infantry formed up before Flauvigny. Within minutes both splendid regiments were reduced to

Battle of Mars-la-Tour, 16 August 1870: situation at 5 p.m.

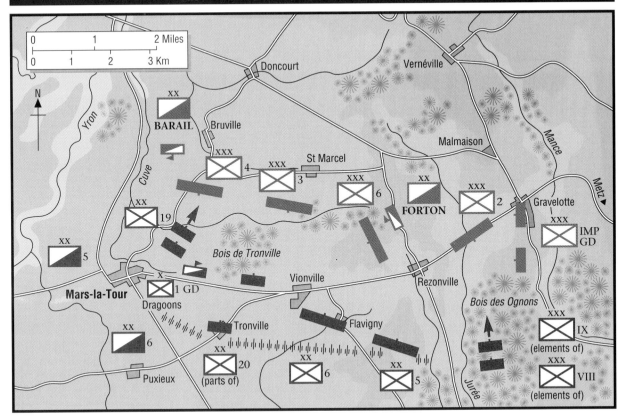

bloodstained heaps. Redern's Brigade pursued the survivors back to the French lines where they briefly involved Bazaine himself in a confined mêlée before they in turn were driven back.

It was now noon and Alvensleben was desperate, with his last infantry reserve halted to the north of Vionville by Canrobert's right in the Tronville woods, and X Corps still to arrive. He still had 5th and 6th Cavalry Divisions uncommitted, however, and he now called upon 12 Brigade's General Bredow of 5th Division to win time. At 2 p.m. the six squadrons of the 7th Cuirassiers and 16th Uhlans swung out north from behind Vionville and, using a depression for concealment, were able to charge into the centre of Canrobert's gun line. The charge poured over and through guns and infantry until halted by Forton's Division which chased the survivors back to the German lines. 'Von Bredow's Death Ride' cost 380 of the original 800 or so, but for the rest of the day, Canrobert's Corps remained stationary sorting out the resulting confusion.

Alvensleben now had to confront the arrival on his left of Ladmirault's IV Corps whose leading division drove the German infantry and cavalry back through Mars-la-Tour on to Tronville. But, as ever, caution overcame the French command and Ladmirault halted before Tronville to bring up his second division, allowing Alvensleben another breathing space. At 3.30 p.m. the first division of X Corps, the 20th under General Kraatz-Koschlau, which had been marching towards the sound of the guns, arrived behind Tronville, part moving through to the woods beyond, as 19th Division under Schwarzkoppen arrived from the west.

While 20th Division shored up the line at Tronville, the 19th emerged blind from Mars-la-Tour in company column, into the heart of Ladmirault's line. Now in extended order, the leading brigade, Wedell's, drove on only to be brought to a bloody halt by the ubiquitous Chassepot: the two regiments, 16th and 57th, lost 2,000 out of 4,600 men within a few minutes.

Then the infantry of Grenier's Division counter-charged and swept the shattered Germans back. At that moment it appeared as if the whole German left would collapse. But once more caution ruled the French command and Ladmirault did nothing to follow-up this success. Meanwhile the senior German officer on the spot, the commander of X Corps, General Voigts-Rhetz, launched the 1st and 2nd Regiments of Dragoon Guards in yet another desperate, time-winning charge. While they were inevitably shot down, they successfully disordered and halted any further French infantry advance upon Mars-la-Tour.

Now the last action of the day on the left developed on the open grass land to the north of Mars-la-Tour, where the German cavalry under Rheinbaben sought to move around Ladmirault's right flank. Three French cavalry divisions countered this and a massive mêlée developed between more than forty-nine squadrons of dragoons, Uhlans, hussars and chasseurs. While

the French were pushed back towards Bruville, both sides were left in utter confusion and by 7 p.m. they had mutually drawn apart.

As the sun set the fighting died down around Mars-la-Tour only to spring up briefly again to the east, south of Rezonville where parts of IX Corps and First Army's VIII Corps had arrived on the field. Frederick Charles, only belatedly realizing like Alvensleben earlier, that the entire French Army lay before him, attempted a final decision before nightfall. In the twilight the attack was highly successful, with the French troops before Rezonville being thrown back and German cavalry getting amongst their panic-swept ranks. But in the pitch dark the attack ground to a halt and the firing at last came to an end.

The fighting had been desperate for the Germans with two corps holding the entire French Army at a cost of under 15,800 against some 17,000 for the French. Yet they had successfully held the Verdun road thereby cutting the line of French retreat. Bazaine, although as

◄ *The Battle of Mars-la-Tour is possibly best remembered for the 'Ride of Death', by General Bredow's 12 Brigade. The commitment of a single brigade of cavalry to 'win time' was an act of desperation yet it succeeded in disrupting the deployment of Canrobert's VI Corps at a crucial point in the afternoon. The 7th Magdeburg Cuirassier Regiment led the charge through the gun-line of VI Corps before being counter-charged by Forton's Cavalry Division. Their success reflected the poverty of French artillery as much as their own determination. They left half their number behind, but their path was marked by a trail of death and destruction. (ASKB)*

ever displaying great bravery on the field, had not only allowed this, but had let slip an ideal opportunity to destroy Second Army piecemeal. As evening fell Bazaine had to contend with absolute confusion behind the lines as the civilians on the road panicked back to Metz, while several of his corps would need time to reassemble after the day's fighting. Rather than risk further fighting the next day and with his artillery commander General Soleille informing him that it would take twenty-four hours to obtain the necessary replenishments of ammunition from Metz, Bazaine ordered a short retreat.

As morning broke on the 17th, the French Army found itself falling back towards Metz to a line between St-Privat and Rezonville. If anything, the confusion was greater than ever before as battalions and squadrons marched back over their own supply lines. Many men, without food or ammunition, just helped themselves from the wagons, leaving the Intendants little idea as to what supplies would be available when official

indents were received. Further, many wounded men were simply left at Rezonville to be treated by German army doctors.

For Moltke, news of Mars-la-Tour confirmed that he had the entire Army of the Rhine at his mercy. It was obvious from the battle reports that Bazaine was more concerned about his communications with Metz than with any thoughts of cutting his way through to Verdun. Even if Bazaine did attempt either to push through to Mars-la-Tour or take the more northern routes through Doncourt or St-Privat, he would be inviting attack on the road. Confident that Bazaine would in fact retire upon Metz, Moltke's orders for the 17th directed all corps of Second Army to swing north-east. While the battered III and X Corps spent the 17th resting on the previous day's battlefield alongside the intact VIII and IX Corps, the remainder of Second Army marched up from their crossing points at Pont-à-Mousson and Corny to join them by nightfall. Meanwhile Moltke kept a tight rein on Steinmetz, being rightly wary of his insubordination and impetuosity. He was to provide the pivot for Moltke's grand pinning movement for the 18th and consequently not only was Steinmetz strictly ordered not to engage in any hostilities, but both I and VIII Corps were removed from his direct command leaving him only VII Corps which crossed the Moselle opposite Ars just south of Metz on the 17th.

During the 17th, while the large dust clouds of the retreating French readily revealed to Moltke that they were falling back directly on Metz, he was none the less without any detailed reconnaissance. The German cavalry had yet to recover from the previous day's fighting and fresh mounted formations were not available until nightfall. Consequently as Moltke prepared his orders for the 18th he was unaware that Bazaine's army had settled on a strong defensive position between St-Privat to the north and the Rozérieulles plateau overlooking the Moselle to the south. Hence, when he ordered First and Second Army forward in the early hours of the 18th, he was unaware that five French corps were in a strong defensive position at a right angle to his projected line of advance.

◀ *Although not as famous Bredow's charge, the action of the 1st and 2nd Guard Dragoon Regiments was almost as important. Despite heavy loss they managed to charge into the head of Grenier's and Cissey's Divisions, thereby halting what might have turned into a successful French counter-attack on the German left. (*Illustrated London News*)*

▶ *Private, Hesse-Darmstadt Infantry, Regiment No. 1. The army of the North German Confederation contained many non-Prussian contingents of whom the Hessen contingent were typical. Since 1849 their uniforms and equipment had followed that of Prussian army in general cut and design, although with a number of distinctive features. The* **pickelhaube** *was higher and carried a Hessen lion plate, while white lace* **lutzens** *adorned the collar, and the cuffs were pointed. Illustration by Les Still.*

◀ *The Battle of Mars-la-Tour ended with history's last great classic cavalry mêlée between some forty-five squadrons of dragoons, Uhlans, hussars and chasseurs. Although the outcome of the clash went to the Germans, the action was peripheral to the main battle, with darkness falling before any decisive conclusion could be reached. (ASKB)*

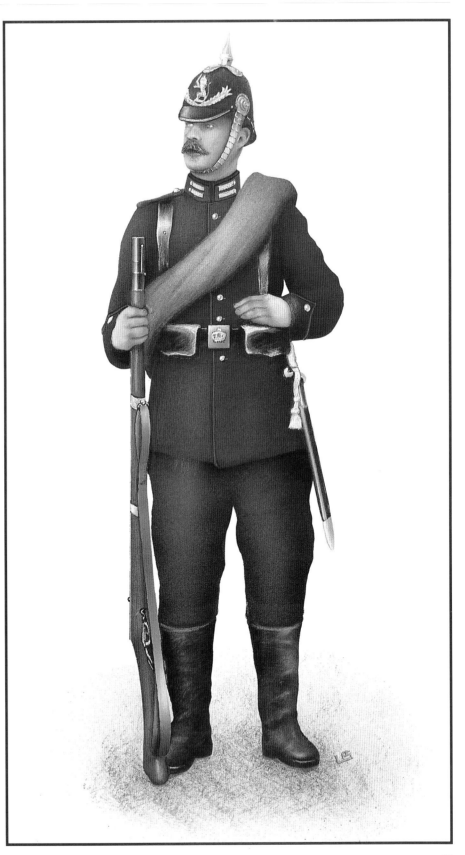

THE BATTLE OF
GRAVELOTTE–ST-PRIVAT

The Position

Bazaine had decided on the formidable position that his army now occupied on the night of the 16th as an appropriate location, just outside the ring of forts around Metz. The line dominated the valley approaches to Metz from which the Germans would emerge while still being only a mile from the security of the forts. The eight to nine mile length of the position resembled a hog's back, with gentle slopes in the north becoming steeper towards the centre and south. The

◀ *This view of Metz from the north gives an idea of the city's size. Its vast stores of ammunition and food, and its encircling forts, offered a logical point to concentrate the Army of the Rhine prior to retreat towards Châlons, but was to prove a critical bottle-neck for the various corps, imposing a crucial delay on the retreat. (*Illustrated London News*)*

◀ *The population of Metz were treated to the spectacle of German prisoners being escorted through the streets prior to the city's investment. They were possibly the only people in France to witness such a sight. (*Illustrated London News*)*

northern end of the line was anchored in the well-built village of St-Privat which commanded the surrounding slopes with an excellent field of fire across the bare fields. Moving south to the village of Amanvillers, the position looked down a gentle slope whose field of fire was tailor-made for the Chassepot and mitrailleuse. The position then changed in nature somewhat to the south of Amanvillers with the thickly wooded Bois de Genivaux covering the northern end of the Mance Ravine. The remainder of the French line running south followed the Mance stream, whose course had cut a deep ravine, to join the Moselle at Ars. The steep slopes of the ravine were thickly wooded although the floor was flat and treeless, and pitted with small quarries and gravel pits. A third of the way down its length the Gravelotte–St-Hubert road crossed the ravine on a raised causeway. To the east of the Mance Ravine was the Rozérieulles plateau whose slopes swung round to the south-east just above the River Moselle. At the southern end, the Bois des Ognon and Bois de Vaux covered the west and east banks of the Mance respectively, the Bois de Vaux also covering the south-eastern slopes of the Rozérieulles plateau. Back in the centre of this line, sitting above the Mance Ravine were three walled farms: Moscow, Leipzig and St-Hubert. The solid walls of these provided natural fortresses with which to anchor the French line. Finally, the farmstead on the heights of the Point du Jour overlooked the south-eastern slopes down to the Mance.

Bazaine's army should have had most of the 17th to settle into this formidable position, but, as ever, the familiar confusion of march routes meant that most corps had not reached their positions until near nightfall, having taken much of the day to march three to four miles. At the northern end of the line around St-Privat stood Canrobert's VI Corps with its right flank at Roncourt and its left in the farm buildings of Jerusalem. It deployed a strong advance guard of two infantry regiments at Ste-Marie-aux-Chênes, a mile to the west of St-Privat. Next was Ladmirault's IV Corps drawn up from the farm of Jerusalem through Amanvillers and down to Montigny, both villages on the western face of the ridge. Leboeuf's III Corps

held the long crest of the Rozérieulles plateau to the south, from La Folie to St-Hubert. A brigade of III Corps was forward of this in the Bois de Genivaux. To the left of III Corps was Frossard's II Corps covering the remainder of the plateau's crest from St-Hubert to its southern end overlooking the Moselle, the Point du Jour. Its advance posts held the woods and quarries of the Mance Ravine. Finally, the southern flank was held by Lapasset's Brigade (detached from Failly's V Corps) which was deployed in the villages of Vaux and Jussy at the foot of the Rozérieulles plateau. Two miles to the rear of the centre-left stood the two forts of Plappeville and St-Quentin which commanded the main roads back into Metz. Between these forts stood the massed ranks of Bourbaki's Imperial Guards Corps and the Army's artillery reserve, with almost the entire cavalry crammed into the Châtel valley half-way between the Guard and III Corps. The cavalry were to play almost no part in the forthcoming battle. Finally, Bazaine established his headquarters in Fort Plappeville, more than two miles from the nearest point on the front and more than six miles from St-Privat to the north.

The night of the 17th and morning of the 18th were spent digging trenches and rifle-pits, loop-holing farm walls and buildings, and even camouflaging artillery and *mitrailleuse* positions. The exception to this 'digging-in' was Canrobert's VI Corps who had lost most of their entrenching tools. In choosing this position and making his dispositions, defence and a safe passage for retreat back to Metz were foremost in Bazaine's mind. This helps explain why his northern flank rested on thin air while the central and south were immensely strong with the Guard behind them: Bazaine intended to fight a defensive action. The thought that the position might offer a springboard for a decisive counter-attack does not appear to have crossed his mind.

Moltke's Plan of Attack

On the 17th, as he considered the situation from Royal headquarters at Flavigny, Moltke knew that the French Army lay somewhere to his east. But apart from reports throughout the day from VII

THE BATTLE OF GRAVELOTTE–ST-PRIVAT

German advance on morning of 18 August 1870: situation at 8 a.m. as seen from the south

German forces:
SECOND ARMY
A 12th Cavalry Division (XII Corps)
B 23rd Division (XII Corps)
C 24th Division (XII Corps)
D Guard Cavalry Division (Guards Corps)
E 1st Guards Division (Guards Corps)
F 2nd Guards Division (Guards Corps)

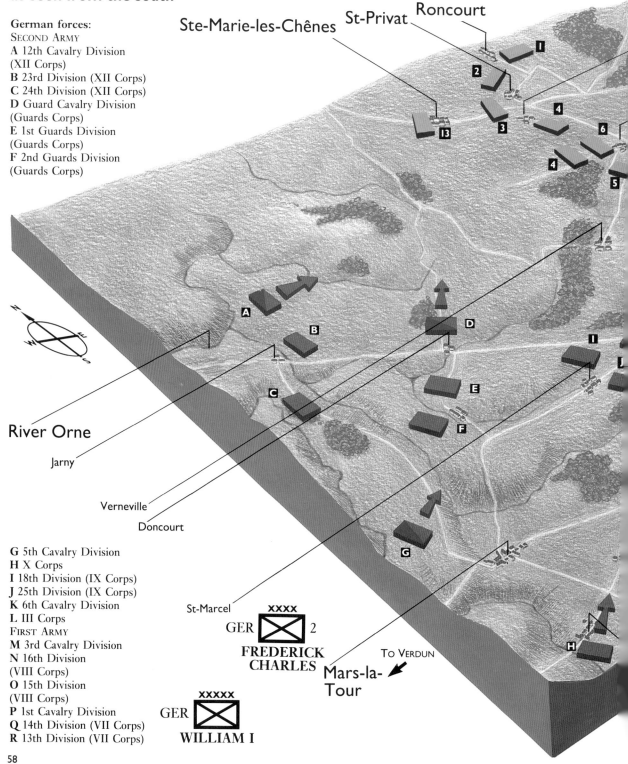

G 5th Cavalry Division
H X Corps
I 18th Division (IX Corps)
J 25th Division (IX Corps)
K 6th Cavalry Division
L III Corps
FIRST ARMY
M 3rd Cavalry Division
N 16th Division (VIII Corps)
O 15th Division (VIII Corps)
P 1st Cavalry Division
Q 14th Division (VII Corps)
R 13th Division (VII Corps)

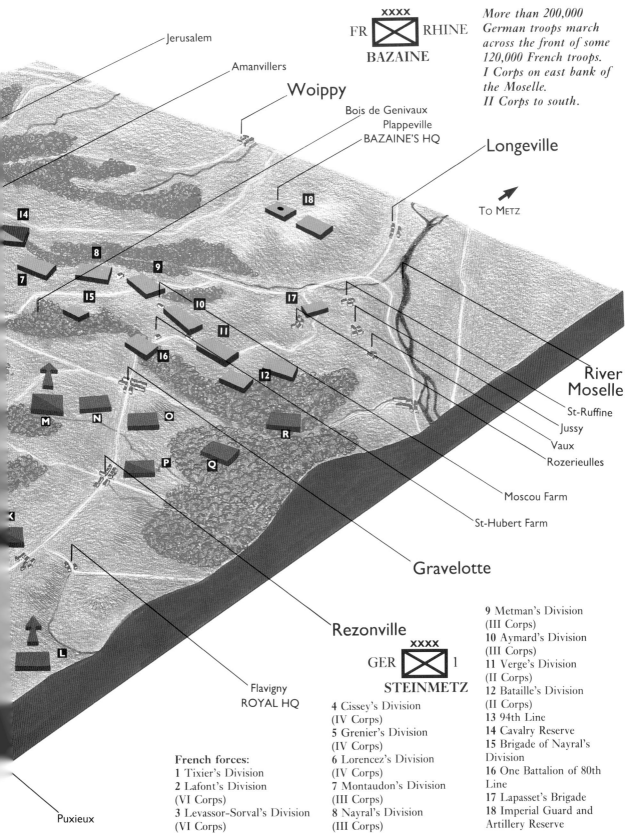

Jerusalem

Amanvillers

FR ⊠ RHINE
XXXX
BAZAINE

More than 200,000 German troops march across the front of some 120,000 French troops. I Corps on east bank of the Moselle. II Corps to south.

Woippy

Bois de Genivaux
Plappeville
BAZAINE'S HQ

Longeville

To Metz

River Moselle

St-Ruffine
Jussy
Vaux
Rozerieulles

Moscou Farm

St-Hubert Farm

Gravelotte

Rezonville

GER ⊠ 1
XXXX
STEINMETZ

Flavigny
ROYAL HQ

Puxieux

4 Cissey's Division
(IV Corps)
5 Grenier's Division
(IV Corps)
6 Lorencez's Division
(IV Corps)
7 Montaudon's Division
(III Corps)
8 Nayral's Division
(III Corps)

French forces:
1 Tixier's Division
2 Lafont's Division
(VI Corps)
3 Levassor-Sorval's Division
(VI Corps)

9 Metman's Division
(III Corps)
10 Aymard's Division
(III Corps)
11 Verge's Division
(II Corps)
12 Bataille's Division
(II Corps)
13 94th Line
14 Cavalry Reserve
15 Brigade of Nayral's Division
16 One Battalion of 80th Line
17 Lapasset's Brigade
18 Imperial Guard and Artillery Reserve

◄ *German field commanders were very much committed to leading from the front. While liable to impulsive actions, which often left their troops exposed, as Manstein demonstrates here, they were willing to brave intense French rifle fire in order to assess the immediate situation and inspire confidence in their men. (ASKB)*

◄ *Below: having begun the action of IX Corps by driving the handful of French defenders from the Château of Vernéville, Manstein based his headquarters in its grounds from noon onwards. Its central location would have been more suitable for the Royal Headquarters rather than the position on the German right where it eventually settled, thereby isolating Moltke from overall tactical control.*

Corps that it was skirmishing with Lapasset's Brigade in the Bois de Vaux, Moltke remained ignorant of the exact location and positions of the body of the French Army. As has been mentioned, this was due to the temporary incapacity of the German cavalry. Moltke assumed that Bazaine would seek to retreat north-west to escape to Verdun, and during the evening of the 17th he made his dispositions based on this faulty, if understandable, assumption.

In effect, Moltke gave orders for a strategic encirclement. Second Army was to advance on a broad front from its positions between Mars-la-Tour and Rezonville on a north-eastern angle. The Guard and XII Corps were to be at the northern end of this, passing through Doncourt and ready to swing east or west as the circumstances demanded. IX Corps, supported by X and III Corps in reserve was to the Guard's right, passing through Vionville either to pin the French or support the Guard and Saxons as matters developed. Frederick Charles was ordered to attack the French when and where contact was made, and he was given full discretion as to how he would handle this. First Army was to remain static so as to act as a pivot for Second Army: of its three corps, I was still on the east bank of the Moselle around Courcelles to cover any French sortie from Metz. VIII and VII Corps were deployed in the Bois de Vaux with the objective of pinning II Corps around the Point du Jour, which Moltke assumed was a rearguard. Given that only VII Corps was still under Steinmetz's direct control, Moltke felt he had little room to make mischief. Finally, II Corps, still many miles to the south-west, was to march up to arrive behind First Army late on the afternoon of the 18th.

At sunrise on the 18th the massed ranks of Moltke's army moved off to discover the French and destroy them. What they did not realize was that their march route took them at an angle of 45 degrees across the front of an entrenched French Army. As the sun rose higher they were soon to discover their error, but Moltke was to prove powerless to prevent his subordinate army commanders reacting in a near-disastrous manner.

The German Advance

From 7 to 8 a.m. a solid phalanx of more than 200,000 men was advancing on a front of some eight miles, inclining north-east, driving across country almost regardless of terrain. By 9 a.m. Leboeuf could report to Bazaine the vast dust-clouds raised by this host. Bazaine acknowledged the information and instructed Leboeuf to sit tight, dismissing any suggestion of striking at the exposed flank of Second Army. A similar order issued by Royal headquarters to Steinmetz was to elicit a far less obedient response.

At about 10 a.m. Frederick Charles began to make out the white tent lines on the Amanvillers ridge around Montigny. As Moltke's instructions had led him to believe that the French were retreating northwards, Frederick Charles assumed that he had found the French rear-guard's flank. Like Alvensleben on the 16th, he felt it his duty to attack immediately without the benefit of reconnaissance or reference to Moltke.

At 10.15 a.m. he ordered the entire Second Army to turn east. Meanwhile Moltke too had been reassessing the reports coming in and at 10.30 he issued orders for an attack on Bazaine's line, but he was working on a different assumption from that of Frederick Charles. Moltke now believed that the entire French Army was drawn up south of Amanvillers and

consequently initiated his plan to encircle them; like Frederick Charles he too dispensed with any additional reconnaissance. Unfortunately, what Frederick Charles thought was the French rear-guard and what Moltke thought was the right was in fact the French centre, with IV and VI Corps stretching away to the north.

Moltke ordered both First and Second Armies to attack. Steinmetz was to push forward through Gravelotte to maintain pressure on the French left while IX Corps was to continue eastwards towards Vernéville as ordered by Frederick Charles. The rest of Second Army was to swing north-east towards Amanvillers to envelop what Moltke thought was the French right flank. By 11.45 these orders were being executed when news reached Frederick Charles that French troops had been identified at St-Privat. Realizing that the bulk of Second Army would have to move much further to the north to outflank the French successfully, orders were dispatched to Manstein, commander of IX Corps to delay his attack. It was too late and just before 12 noon, the battle opened as the artillery of IX Corps deployed east of Vernéville without infantry support and opened fire.

Manstein, like Alvensleben on the 16th, had been driving forward without reconnaissance since 10.15 a.m. He massed 54 guns just north-east of Vernéville and opened fire. He was immediately answered by the full weight of Ladmirault's Corps artillery from less than 1,000 yards. The French infantry, until then still sitting in their tents and cooking lunch, poured forward to occupy their rifle-pits and trenches. Manstein now discovered that he had unwittingly made a salient for himself with VI Corps to his left and III Corps to his right, while his leading infantry were still marching up behind Vernéville. With his artillery within Chassepot and *mitrailleuse* range, his gunners were devastated. For an hour the Hessian gunners withstood the hail of shells and bullets, but at 1 p.m. Manstein ordered them to fall back. Eight guns remained for a time at the corner of the Bois de Genivaux to cover the retreat and some troops of Grenier's Division seized the opportunity to rush forward and capture two guns. Only a desperate charge by the fusilier

◀ *Commander of IV Corps, General de Ladmirault held the line south of St-Privat. His men were the first to see action on the 18th with the advance by Manstein of his unsupported artillery. Although Manstein's isolated corps invited counter-attack, Ladmirault did nothing to exploit the situation. Later in the day, though, he must take credit for stabilizing the right flank when VI Corps collapsed at St-Privat. (ASKB)*

battalion of the 85th Regiment saved the rest although it lost twelve officers and 400 men within a few minutes.

At this juncture IX Corps was highly vulnerable as its shattered gunners fell back on the infantry of its 18th and 25th Divisions just emerging from Vernéville; the two Hessian divisions were confronting a full French corps without any immediate support to either left or right yet Ladmirault sat tight. He had not informed Bazaine until 12.30 that he was closely engaged with the Germans and when he did Bazaine failed to react in any way. Sitting at Plappeville Bazaine seemed content to allow the Germans to smash themselves into his line without any reaction. In fact, not only was Bazaine to remain at Plappeville throughout the battle, but he did not dispatch a single aide

◀ *At midday on the 18th Manstein deployed the Hessian artillery of the 25th Infantry Division east of Vernéville in what was an exposed salient before Ladmirault's main position. The gunners were soon losing men to French rifle fire, and had to be drawn back to safer positions as their infantry arrived. (ASKB)*

◀ *The 18th and 25th Hessian Divisions moved up east of Vernéville to find themselves the target of both IV and III Corps. Throughout the early afternoon they held their isolated position despite heavy casualties and the danger of French counter-attack. (ASKB)*

▶ *Gunner, Prussian Foot Artillery. The German artillery played a key role in countering the entrenched French positions with well directed fire from their Krupp guns. Their uniforms were distinguished by black collar and cuffs edged in red piping and a ball-top (**kugel***) to their* **pickelhaube** *helmets. They were armed with short artillery hangers and carbines. Illustration by Les Still.*

◀ *In an attempt to improve their exposed position, the Hessian infantry stormed the farm buildings of Champenois before Amanvillers despite heavy loss. Later in the day this toe-hold on the slope below Amanvillers provided a jumping-off point to seize the village as St-Privat fell to the Guard. As would be a familiar pattern all day, Ladmirault's men made no effort to retake the farm despite its exposed position. (ASKB)*

forward to assess the situation. Instead he relied on his corps commanders to react to each German thrust and to report on the result. Throughout most of the 18th the bulk of Bazaine's staff was to engage itself in arranging promotions and awards for the action of the 16th!

Given a breathing space, Manstein quickly shored up his position. The 18th Division was moved forward to his right to the various farmsteads on the northern edge of the Bois de Genivaux. On his left he sent 25th Division to the edge of the Bois de la Cusse while he brought forward every available gun. By 2.00 p.m., with the arrival of the 3 Guard Brigade and the batteries of III Corps, Manstein's line stabilized. Throughout the remainder of the afternoon the artillery of both sides maintained a fierce exchange but Manstein had not the strength to push his infantry forward. Ladmirault's men were well dug in on a ridge which dominated the line of German approach and the Chassepot and *mitrailleuse* ruled out frontal assault. Stalemate ensued.

Just after noon, when Moltke heard the guns of IX Corps, he and the king rode forward from Flavigny to Rezonville. While this made the German HQ more accessible it still denied it any view of the German right. Yet Moltke did not expect any significant fighting there as Steinmetz was again ordered to sit tight with VII Corps, as was Goeben, his VIII Corps still being under the

direct control of the Royal HQ. Unfortunately for Moltke this availed him nothing as both Steinmetz and Goeben would ignore their specific orders.

At noon First Army sat astride the Mance Ravine in the woods covering each side. Farthest east was 26 Brigade of 13th Division at Jussy and St-Ruffine, facing the French at Rozérieulles. The other brigade of 13th Division and the whole of 14th Division were deployed in the Bois de Vaux and Bois des Ognons. Coming round to the north-west was 16th Division of VIII Corps at Gravelotte with 18th Division to their left, then, at a little distance, stood 15th Division in the Bois de Gerivaux. Finally, 1st Cavalry Division was deployed around the village of Malmaison. Coming round before VII and VIII Corps lay the whole of Frossard's II Corps and the left of Leboeuf's III Corps well entrenched on the Rozérieulles plateau.

Frossard's position was a veritable fortress: the crest dominated the plain below with the Mance Ravine acting as a moat while the thick woods on the slopes of the ravine itself obstructed German movements and the further slopes up to the crest were bare and a natural killing ground. Frossard's engineering background had ensured that the crest was criss-crossed by a series of trenches, rifle-pits, gun-emplacements and loopholed walls.

Although Steinmetz ought only to have had authority over VII Corps, Goeben's VIII Corps

▶ *The road between Gravelotte and St-Hubert crossed the fateful Mance Ravine on a raised causeway and provided the focal point for VIII Corp's assaults. This contemporary picture shows the wooded lower slopes of the Mance Ravine which then gave way to the bare upper slopes - an ideal killing ground for Frossard's rifles. Steinmetz duly provided the targets.* **(Battles of the Nineteenth Century***)*

being under the direct authority of the king, it appears that at about midday Steinmetz unilaterally re-assumed authority over it. At the same moment he decided that as the man on the spot his judgment as to what action to take overrode the specific order to do nothing, this despite the fact that he was well aware of Moltke's strategic plan, having been present the day before when it was drawn up. Hearing the firing to the north, he decided to initiate a full-scale attack by First Army. By 1 p.m. he had deployed the 150 guns available to him on either side of Gravelotte.

Meanwhile Weltzien's 15th Division drove forward to clear the Bois de Genivaux and link up with Manstein's 18th Division to its left (this action was the decision of VIII Corps' commander, Goeben, not Steinmetz). As they moved into the woods they soon lapped up against a solid abatis built by Metman's Division and were met by a wall of Chassepot fire. Simultaneously the guns around Moscow and St-Hubert poured fire onto them and the leading battalions were brought to a halt.

Steinmetz, who had not ordered this, none the less felt it was the right direction to be heading, towards the French. His own artillery around Gravelotte was too far from the French positions to bring an adequate weight of fire to bear so he decided they needed to be brought to the western edge of the Mance Ravine. As this would bring the gunners within range of the French infantry

▲ *General Frossard, Commander of II Corps was one of the more able senior French commanders. His background as an engineer officer, is reflected in the intensive 'digging-in' by his men at both Spicheren and the Point du Jour. His extensive and well-conceived defences proved capable of defeating all attacks and gave the Chassepot an excellent field of fire as well as considerable protection from the German artillery. (ASKB)*

▲ *The Commander of VIII Corps, General Goeben, proved a worthy subordinate to his reckless Army Commander, Steinmetz. Despite knowing his corps was no longer under Steinmetz's immediate control, he accepted the order to commit his men to inevitable destruction in assaulting the French position. Throughout the afternoon of the 18th he raised hardly a single objection as he committed brigade after brigade at the behest of*

Battle of Gravelotte St-Privat: situation at 1-2 p.m.

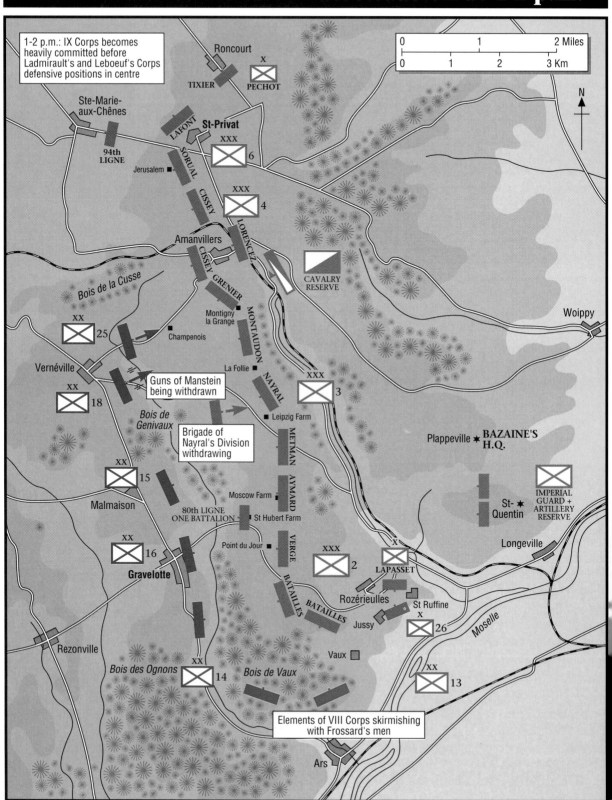

1-2 p.m.: IX Corps becomes heavily committed before Ladmirault's and Leboeuf's Corps defensive positions in centre

Roncourt

x
PECHOT

TIXIER

Ste-Marie-aux-Chênes

LAFONT

St-Privat

94th LIGNE

SORUAL

XXX
6

Jerusalem ■

CISSEY

XXX
4

LORENCEZ

Amanvillers

CISSEY

CAVALRY RESERVE

Bois de la Cusse

GRENIER

Woippy

XX
25

Montigny la Grange

MONTAUDON

Champenois ■

Vernéville

La Follie ■

NAYRAL

XXX
3

XX
18

Guns of Manstein being withdrawn

Bois de Genivaux

■ Leipzig Farm

Plappeville ★ **BAZAINE'S H.Q.**

Brigade of Nayral's Division withdrawing

METMAN

XX
15

Moscow Farm

AYMARD

St- ★ Quentin

IMPERIAL GUARD + ARTILLERY RESERVE

Malmaison

80th LIGNE ONE BATTALION

■ St Hubert Farm

XX
16

Point du Jour ■

VERGE

XXX
2

x
LAPASSET

Longeville

Gravelotte

BATAILLES

BATAILLES

Rozérieulles

St Ruffine

Jussy

x
26

Moselle

Rezonville

XX
14

Vaux ■

Bois des Ognons

Bois de Vaux

XX
13

Elements of VIII Corps skirmishing with Frossard's men

Ars

0   1   2 Miles
0   1   2   3 Km

N

lug in on the eastern side of the ravine, Steinmetz, at just after 2 p.m., ordered 15th and 6th Divisions of VIII Corps forward to clear the way for his artillery.

By 2.00 p.m. Moltke had lost control of the battle. This was partly his own fault for remaining too long at the isolated hamlet of Flavigny which placed him as far back from the German front as Bazaine at Plappeville was from the French. Essentially, by early afternoon, both commanders were directing, if Bazaine's conduct can be so described, their respective armies by remote control, without any sight of the actual fighting. Even when he had moved forward to Rezonville, Moltke's physical view of the German right was almost non-existent and it placed him six miles from the German left where his master-plan was meant to reach fruition. Further, both Steinmetz and Goeben had consciously decided to ignore Moltke's order to remain passive, an order that was repeated at 1.00 p.m. Moltke's strategic plan to pin Bazaine's left while outflanking his right was to come rapidly unstuck as the afternoon progressed — the additional length of Bazaine's line to the north meant the enveloping movement would take far longer than expected. Meanwhile the south of Moltke's line was about to commit suicide.

First Army's Attack

At just before 2.30 p.m. Steinmetz ordered VIII Corps forward across the ravine. While Goeben's assault with elements of 15th Division had been bloodily halted, for Steinmetz it had simply fuelled his belief in this course of action. The objective of VIII Corps' assault was the farm of St-Hubert which would provide a foothold on the Rozérieulles plateau. It would also provide cover from Chassepot fire so that his artillery could move up to the edge of the ravine. Of Goeben's Corps, the whole of 15th Division and 31 Brigade of 16th Division moved forward frontally to assault the farm.

The farm buildings sat just below the top of the ridge and commanded the steep eastern slope of the ravine. Above and to each side of the farm were the main trench lines of II and III Corps and

the farm would have to be taken before any assault on these could be contemplated. The farm itself was held by a single battalion of the 80th Regiment of Aymard's Division.

The three German brigades moved forward across the bottom of the ravine, 15th Division passing to either side of the causeway carrying the Gravelotte to St-Hubert road across the ravine, with 31 Brigade in support. As they crossed the stream a hail of bullets and shells smashed into their ranks. As they moved up the lower slopes, the thick undergrowth, trees and quarries broke up the company columns of 29 and 30 Brigades. Despite this, they managed to move up the slope to occupy the gravel-pits directly below the heights of the Point du Jour and St-Hubert, with 31 Brigade moving in behind. But from here they could move no further as the rifles and guns of Frossard's Corps swept the area and their shattered ranks sought what cover they could in the pits and trees.

In this exposed and tenuous position, a localized French counter-attack would have swept all three brigades away, yet neither Frossard nor Leboeuf stirred. Instead, all their guns' attention being drawn to the eastern slope, Steinmetz was able to bring forward his 150 guns from around Gravelotte to the western edge of the ravine by 3 p.m. Within a few minutes the farm of St-Hubert was a blazing ruin and the garrison was slaughtered. By 3.30 the survivors of the 80th had to retire to the main trench line just above the farm, and elements of three German units, 8th Jäger and 60th and 67th Infantry Regiments dashed forward to seize the ruins. The guns then began pounding the trenches and guns of Frossard's Corps thereby discouraging any thought of a counter-attack to retake the German toe-hold in the ruined farm.

Steinmetz was elated and reported back to the king that he had seized the heights. The reality was that the farm of St-Hubert was a death-trap overlooked by a complex of trenches and the massed guns of the two French corps. From Moscow Farm on its left and the Point du Jour on its right, all avenues of advance were covered. All attempts by the men of VIII Corps to move beyond its walls were met by a wall of bullets and

◀ *Like many other regiments of VII Corps, the 39th Fusilier Regiment suffered severe losses during the afternoon assault on the Point du Jour. They rallied on the main gun-line at the western edge of the Mance Ravine whose proximity to the opposite ridge is demonstrated by the fact that their needle-guns were within extreme range of Frossard's trenches. They held this position until fighting ceased at nightfall. (ASKB)*

◀ *The determination of the German infantry regardless of loss and the impossibility of their task saw many small groups push forward through a hail of bullets and shell. It is doubtful that the surviving officers had so suicidally exposed themselves.* (Battles of the Nineteenth Century)

shell. But Steinmetz, pre-empting the generals of the Western Front forty-five years later, believed that by feeding in just a few more men victory could be seized. It ought to be said that Goeben, whose corps was now being massacred, did now challenge Steinmetz's view but Steinmetz was the senior and he still had VII Corps, undisputably under his command, to order forward.

As if to draw Steinmetz forward, at 4 p.m. the French batteries fell silent as they needed to replenish their ammunition. They also wished to reduce their visibility from the increasingly accurate and destructive fire of the German guns now established on the western edge of the ravine. Steinmetz construed this as proof that his interpretation was correct and he launched VII Corps forward against the untouched Point du Jour. Initially 26 Brigade of 13th Division made a diversionary attack from Ars. This succeeded in taking the villages of Vaux and Jussy from Lapasset's Brigade, but attempts at a further advance towards St-Ruffine were halted and this

▶ *On the morning of 18 August only General Zastrow's VII Corps remained under the direct command of Steinmetz. Having already demonstrated his willingness for aggressive assault at Spicheren, Zastrow willingly committed his divisions to the assault on the Point du Jour. By evening half his corps lay dead or wounded before Frossard's position. (ASKB)*

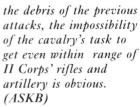

attack petered out. This isolated advance by a German brigade of two regiments had one unforeseen impact for the Germans: it helped reinforce Bazaine's fear for his precious communications with Metz. While the various German corps and army commanders were doing their best to offer Bazaine opportunities to destroy them piecemeal, Bazaine's attention was firmly focused on a non-existent German threat to his southern lines of retreat.

As the firing on the extreme right died down and the flames from the burning farms of St-Hubert and Moscow on the left grew higher, the commander of VII Corps, General Zastrow, now proved to be a worthy subordinate to Steinmetz. His 25 and 28 Brigades were deployed in the Bois de Vaux with 27 Brigade as the reserve south of Gravelotte. Just before 4 p.m. 25 and 28 Brigades moved forward against Verge's Division's entrenched infantry of Frossard's Corps around the Point du Jour. Initially the wooded lower slopes gave them some protection, but as the skirmishers emerged at the wood line they were immediately hit by a wall of Chassepot, *mitrailleuse* and artillery fire. The bulk of the two brigades were meanwhile advancing in dense company column but before they could close the tree line their ranks were swept into confusion by the broken remnants of the skirmishers. Within a few minutes utter disorder reigned at the base of the ravine as both brigades joined the previous survivors. Steinmetz now capped this folly by launching an entire division of cavalry forward to

▲ *This contemporary picture of the road up to St-Hubert crossing the Mance Ravine illustrates the narrowness of the path that 1st Cavalry Division had to traverse. If one takes account of the debris of the previous attacks, the impossibility of the cavalry's task to get even within range of II Corps' rifles and artillery is obvious. (ASKB)*

throw themselves on the retreating enemy. Quite why Steinmetz thought that Zastrow's assault had succeeded and that the French were retreating is unclear: the charitable interpretation is that the dense smoke and confusion deceived him. More likely his characteristic impetuosity and reckless disregard for losses blinded him to reason.

Just after 4 p.m. I Corps' 1st Cavalry Division, which till then had been assembled at Malmaison just north of Gravelotte, was ordered forward. It was to follow the road from Gravelotte down across the narrow causeway in the Mance Ravine and then move up through the steep and narrow defile beyond to reach the Rozérieulles plateau. The cavalry were to be followed by the entire VII Corps artillery, part of which limbered up behind the troopers as they moved off. All this was to be executed in clear view of the French on the Point du Jour; folly hardly seems to sum up this action.

It is doubtful if the German infantry crouching in the ravine could believe their eyes as in column of fours the cavalry trotted down the road and then attempted to thread its way round the wagons, limbers and bodies covering the

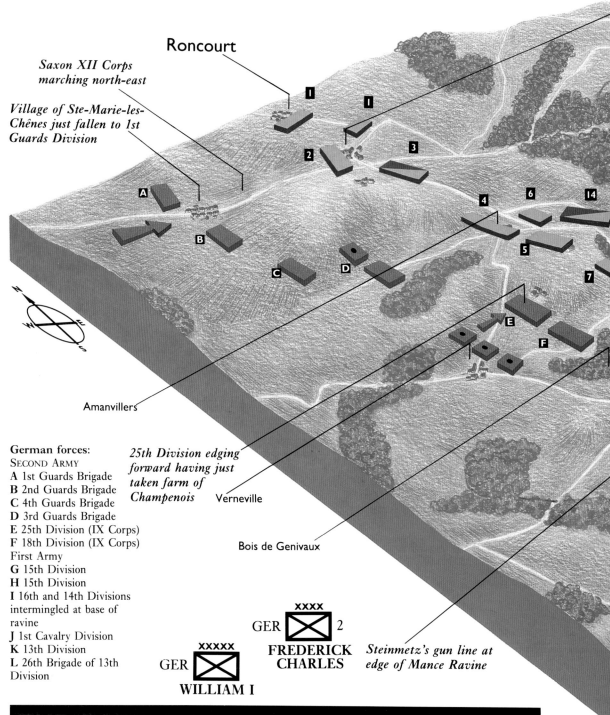

Roncourt

Saxon XII Corps marching north-east

Village of Ste-Marie-les-Chênes just fallen to 1st Guards Division

Amanvillers

25th Division edging forward having just taken farm of Champenois

Verneville

Bois de Genivaux

German forces:
SECOND ARMY
A 1st Guards Brigade
B 2nd Guards Brigade
C 4th Guards Brigade
D 3rd Guards Brigade
E 25th Division (IX Corps)
F 18th Division (IX Corps)
First Army
G 15th Division
H 15th Division
I 16th and 14th Divisions intermingled at base of ravine
J 1st Cavalry Division
K 13th Division
L 26th Brigade of 13th Division

xxxx
GER ⊠ 2
FREDERICK CHARLES

xxxxx
GER ⊠
WILLIAM I

Steinmetz's gun line at edge of Mance Ravine

THE BATTLE OF GRAVELOTTE–ST-PRIVAT

Attack by 1st Cavalry Division across the Mance Ravine and the fall of Ste-Marie-les-Chênes to the Guard, about 4 p.m. 18 August 1870

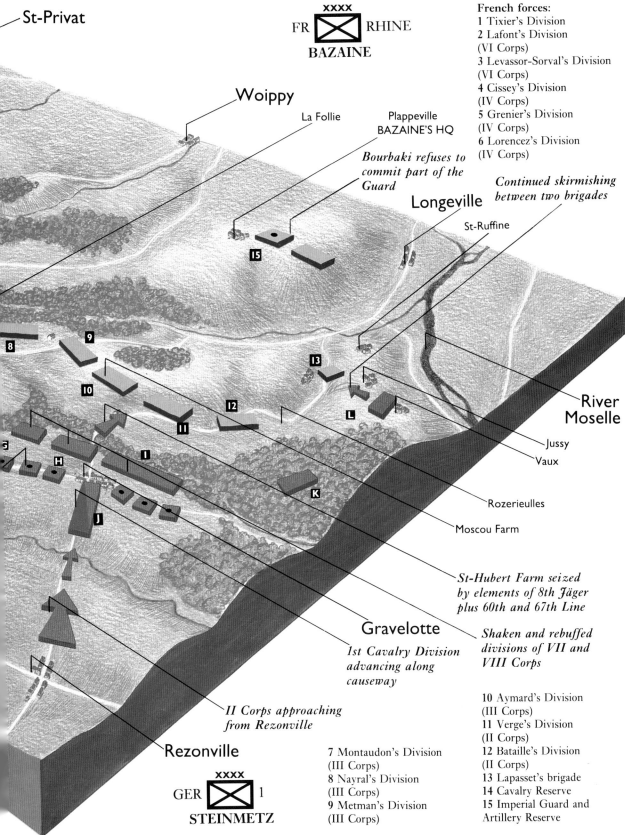

St-Privat

FR ⊠ RHINE
XXXX
BAZAINE

French forces:
1 Tixier's Division
2 Lafont's Division
(VI Corps)
3 Levassor-Sorval's Division
(VI Corps)
4 Cissey's Division
(IV Corps)
5 Grenier's Division
(IV Corps)
6 Lorencez's Division
(IV Corps)

Woippy

La Follie

Plappeville
BAZAINE'S HQ

Bourbaki refuses to commit part of the Guard

Longeville

Continued skirmishing between two brigades

St-Ruffine

River Moselle

Jussy

Vaux

Rozerieulles

Moscou Farm

St-Hubert Farm seized by elements of 8th Jäger plus 60th and 67th Line

Gravelotte

1st Cavalry Division advancing along causeway

Shaken and rebuffed divisions of VII and VIII Corps

II Corps approaching from Rezonville

Rezonville

GER ⊠ 1
XXXX
STEINMETZ

7 Montaudon's Division
(III Corps)
8 Nayral's Division
(III Corps)
9 Metman's Division
(III Corps)

10 Aymard's Division
(III Corps)
11 Verge's Division
(II Corps)
12 Bataille's Division
(II Corps)
13 Lapasset's brigade
14 Cavalry Reserve
15 Imperial Guard and Artillery Reserve

71

◀ *General Fransecky, Commander of II Corps, arrived on the German right late in the afternoon of the 18th to find VII and VIII Corps on the verge of collapse. Incredibly he coolly accepted Steinmetz's direction to commit his 3rd Division to yet another hopeless assault. Before his corps was destroyed, though, he brought the assault to an end and stabilized the line with his 4th Division who held despite the final collapse of First Army. (ASKB)*

causeway while the French guns found their range. Only one cavalry regiment, the 4th Uhlans, managed to thread its way through the debris on the causeway and dash up to deploy on the plateau to the right of the road. Within minutes half their number were shot down and the survivors streamed back to seek what cover they could in the gravel-pits. Meanwhile, four artillery batteries managed to cross the obstacles on the causeway to reach the edge of the plateau by 4.30 p.m. Two of these batteries were shot down before they could unlimber, a few survivors joining the jumble at the bottom of the ravine. The other two did manage to get into action, one on the tree line, the other behind the walls of St-Hubert. Despite being subjected to murderous fire, both batteries valiantly remained in action during the next two hours, the one at St-Hubert being reduced to a single gun by nightfall.

As the men of both VII and VIII Corps strove to present as small a target as possible at the base of the Mance Ravine, Steinmetz pondered his next move. For all the previous sacrifices, his recklessness had succeeded only in achieving an exposed salient at St-Hubert with two corps of First Army on the verge of collapse. Yet Bazaine did nothing to take advantage of this. Initially, as Steinmetz's attack had developed, Bazaine had ordered Bourbaki to detach a brigade of voltigeurs from the Guard to support Frossard, and one of

General Deligny's moved a little forward. Bourbaki had correctly challenged this pointless depletion of the reserve and Bazaine had immediately rescinded the order, instead directing Bourbaki to act as he saw fit. Bazaine's deferment to Bourbaki's challenge not only illustrates his lack of determination to fill the role of a commander-in-chief, but his recognition of Bourbaki's higher social standing.

In fact, by mid-afternoon Bourbaki had an excellent opportunity to split First and Second Armies. The Guard and XII Corps of Second Army were still marching north-east to get around the flank of VI Corps while the bulk of First Army crouched in the Mance Ravine. Between the two was only IX Corps pinned below Amanvillers and Montigny with a considerable gap to each side. But Moltke was in no danger for Bazaine's only concern was to secure his line of retreat into Metz. Further, at this stage, none of his corps commanders ventured to suggest that the Guard, reserve cavalry and artillery massed between Plappeville and Jussy could be used for anything more dramatic than to support the continuing defence.

Just after 4.30 p.m. Steinmetz, having considered the situation and concerned that his assault was flagging as the gunfire died down, appealed directly to the king at Malmaison to allow him to complete his victory. Although Moltke was at the king's side and was well aware of the crisis in the Mance Ravine, he did and said nothing to intervene in what now occurred. With the nearest fresh reinforcement, Fransecky's II Corps, unable to arrive until at least 7 p.m., Steinmetz asked the king for permission to launch his only two surviving reserve formations, VIII Corps' 32 Brigade and VII Corps' 27 Brigade forward. Steinmetz insisted that his tenuous hold on the plateau at St-Hubert was in fact a major lodgement and that the French were on the verge of collapse. The king accepted this fiction and Moltke remained silent.

At just after 6 p.m. this pointless action began as both brigades plus three other uncommitted battalions crossed the floor of the ravine. Amid the debris and confusion there, a few other units gathered together in some sort of order and joined the advance up the wooded eastern slope. As they emerged at the wood line they were met by point-blank fire and within minutes were reduced to a bloody shambles. As the men poured back into the ravine, the survivors of the earlier assaults assumed that the French were in close pursuit and joined the flight. Just after 6.30 thousands of men and horses emerged on the western side of the Mance Ravine in total confusion and panic. With French shells landing in their midst, the mass of men and matériel could not be halted much short of Rezonville, even the presence of the king and General Staff being ignored as the multitude fled through Malmaison. As ever, the French remained passive onlookers, Frossard's report to Bazaine bringing forth congratulations on an excellent defence. To be fair, it should be said that in the growing darkness and with the ravine chocked by dead, wounded and destroyed vehicles, it is doubtful whether a French counter-attack could have reached the western side in any degree of order. Ironically the Germans had provided their own defensive barrier.

While the remaining wreckage of VII and VIII Corps milled around the floor of the Mance Ravine, Fransecky's II Corps arrived at Gravelotte at about around 7.00 p.m. Knowing nothing of the afternoon's slaughter and having been placed by the king under Steinmetz's control earlier in the day, Fransecky obeyed orders to continue forward. Neither Moltke nor the king intervened even now as yet another German formation prepared for disaster. Fransecky's leading unit was the 3rd Division which now marched in company column down the western slope, dividing to the left and right of the causeway at the bottom. Picking their way through the debris in the darkness, they began the ascent of the eastern slope only to be met by the now familiar hail of French fire which tore the columns to pieces, inflicting more than 1,300 casualties in a few minutes. At this point the surviving German troops at St-Hubert mistook the leading units of 3rd Division for French and both they and 3rd Division exchanged fire in the dark and confusion. This tragic and pointless slaughter lasted until just before 8 p.m. when the survivors at St-Hubert finally broke and fled back down the slope.

Fransecky himself, now aware of the true situation, ordered 3rd Division to fall back to the base of the ravine where the uncommitted 4th Division provided some support to stabilize the line.

By 10 p.m. all firing had ceased on the line of the Mance Ravine. The French on the plateau had no orders to move forward and the bulk of the German forces before them were mostly shattered fragments, either lying dead on the eastern slope or heading west in chaotic panic. At this stage both Moltke and the king seriously considered ordering a general retreat, but news from the German left and suggestions of a French retreat held their hand. At dawn next day, the men of II Corps' 4th Division were to discover that the French had abandoned the plateau during the night.

The Guard and Saxons at St-Privat

Six miles to the north of the slaughter in the Mance Ravine, the afternoon had seen another German assault on a well-defended position with consequent massive casualties, yet the flank was to provide the Germans with victory.

As Commander of Second Army, Frederick Charles had been responsible in the early hours of the 18th for a delay to the march of the German left. His directions to the Guard and Saxon XII Corps for their respective march routes that morning had failed to note that the two corps would have to cross over if the designated routes were adhered to. As the two corps marched off at about 4 a.m. the Guard had only just left its bivouac at Dieulouard to march through Mars-la-Tour for Doncourt when it had to halt. XII Corps, camped overnight at Pont-à-Mousson, was already passing through Mars-la-Tour on its way to Jussy. This bungle in staff work produced a two-hour delay to the planned flank march around the French right.

The delay only compounded the even greater problem of Moltke's overall intention when at about 10 a.m. it became obvious that the French right extended much farther to the north than had been thought. The original plan for a classic envelopment had assumed that the French extended no further north than Amanvillers.

Hence while Manstein's IX Corps was to pin this down, the Guard and XII Corps was to sweep round via Ste-Marie-aux-Chênes and St-Privat and roll Bazaine up from the north. As has been seen, by midday this plan had come unstuck as Manstein found himself dangerously exposed as he pushed forward his attack, but not on to the French centre. While, by 10 a.m. Frederick Charles knew that Amanvillers was not the French right flank, his failure to order any additional reconnaissance meant that it was not until about 3 p.m. that St-Privat was identified as the actual French right flank.

Through midday and early afternoon the Guard and XII Corps had continued to march north-east. While Manstein fought on the slopes below Amanvillers, Frederick Charles had pushed the Guard through the Bois de la Cusse behind him. Not knowing the extent of Bazaine's line, Ste-Marie-aux-Chênes was still the objective at this stage. As it passed through the Bois de la Cusse Frederick Charles detached 3 Guards Brigade to reinforce Manstein's now hard-pressed Hessians. As has been seen, they were further reinforced by the artillery of III Corps, and in the absence of any serious French counter-attacks Manstein held on into the late afternoon while the Guard and XII Corps marched on.

By 2 p.m. the Guard, marching on the inner track, had reached Habonville at the south-western foot of the slope up to St-Privat. Here they were halted at the order of Frederick Charles to give more time to XII Corps, still marching and sweeping round to the north-east. XII Corps did not approach its objective of Ste-Marie-aux-Chênes until 3 p.m. The village itself was held by the 94th Ligne and a six-gun battery, both of which soon found themselves facing an overwhelming assault. From 2 to 3 p.m. more than 70 guns from the Guards Corps had been deployed in an arc between Habonville and St-Ail and had unleashed a destructive bombardment of the village. just before 3 p.m. 1st Guards Division from the south and 47 Brigade of the Saxon 24th Infantry Division from the north-west swept forward against the village. Yet the 1,500 or so defenders determinedly held on past 3.30 as the needle-gun armed German infantry found it hard

going to close the gap against the Chassepot. Having inflicted considerable loss on both the Guards and Saxons, the 94th Ligne and artillery retreated in good order up the slope to St-Privat covered by the 100th Ligne deployed half-way down the slope. An attempt by the Saxon Brigade to move up the slope in pursuit was driven back by the Chassepots of the 100th into the ruins of Ste-Marie-aux-Chênes.

While the action was progressing, Frederick Charles had at last become aware of the actual extent of the French positions resting at St-Privat. With the assault under way just after 3 p.m., he ordered XII Corps, minus the brigade attacking the village, to recommence their march in a wide arc from Jarny towards the villages of Montois and Roncourt to the north-east. This would finally place XII Corps to the north of Bazaine's line, but it would take them until early evening to cover the additional distance. In the meantime the various brigades of the Guard were drawn up below St-Privat in a line from Ste-Marie-aux-Chênes, south through St-Ail to Habonville. It should be noted that throughout this and well into the afternoon, Moltke with the king, based first at Rezonville and then at Malmaison, played no role in directing the course of events six miles to their north before St-Privat. All actions then and later were to be initiated at the direction of Frederick Charles.

Meanwhile, on the French side Canrobert had had an excellent view of the events unfolding before him since noon. While his position centred on St-Privat was immensely strong, the solid walls of the village and adjacent farms atop the ridge dominating the slopes below, he was concerned at the overall weakness of his corps' situation. A week before, when VI Corps had been rushed from Châlons to Metz, it had left its cavalry division and most of its 4th Infantry Division behind. Further, it was short of artillery as only some sixty of its guns had caught up with it by the 17th, with Bazaine only compensating with a single 12-pounder battery from the vast army reserve on the morning of the 18th. Finally, and possibly most seriously, it had left much of its baggage at Châlons included most of its entrenching tools. While the walls of the village

▶ *Soldier, German line infantry, distinguished by the spiked* **pickelhaube** *and the dark blue red-faced coats adopted by the Prussian army in 1843, and little changed in 27 years; these combined to present the very symbol of Prussian militarism. The infantry went onto action on the 18th in full marching equipment of pack and slung greatcoat, having left their cantonments at Mars-la-Tour that morning expecting a whole day's march before falling on the French. Illustration by Les Still.*

◀ The 57-year-old commander of the Guard Corps, Prince Augustus of Württemberg, does not appear to have questioned his Army Commander's orders to advance across the bare slopes below St-Privat with the élite of the German Army. He was to launch its two divisions, a brigade at a time, to certain destruction by the rifles of VI Corps. (ASKB)

and farms provided cover, Canrobert's men were unable to do much 'digging in'. This was to leave many of VI Corps' men exposed above ground to artillery fire late on the 18th.

As Canrobert watched the Guard massing a mile below at the foot of the slopes up to St-Privat and the more distant columns of XII Corps marching on Roncourt through the middle of the afternoon, he dispatched repeated requests to Bazaine for reinforcments. Apart from ordering Bourbaki to hold his Guard 'ready' to march north, all Bazaine physically sent was some 500 rounds of additional artillery ammunition, sufficient for fifteen minutes' fire. Otherwise Bazaine's attention was fixed on his left, not his right flank. As the afternoon drew on, some 8,000 men of VI Corps prepared to confront about 18,000 men of Prince Augustus' Guard Corps in what was to be a classic demonstration of a contest between flesh and bullets.

The reason why just after 4.30 Frederick Charles ordered the cream of the German Army to march up an open one-mile slope in close order formation is easily explained. Earlier in the day, Moltke's original order to Frederick Charles had been for Second Army to continue its advance to cut the enemy's line of retreat to Verdun and to attack the French 'wherever he may be encountered'! This order had not been revoked and like Steinmetz, Frederick Charles seems to have believed that a determined assault would inevitably succeed; the German offensive spirit and will to win being deemed sufficient to overcome all.

With more than 100 guns now massed in the gun line south of Ste-Marie-aux-Chênes, it might be expected that the weight of artillery fire would have considerably reduced the defenders' ranks, but the fire was poorly directed, falling mainly on the farm buildings of Jerusalem just to the south of St-Privat proper. Meanwhile the guns of XII Corps were now being directed at Roncourt which was held by Pechot's Brigade of Tixier's Division. Few shells at this stage were actually falling on St-Privat and the prone ranks of VI Corps in and around it.

The Guard Corps was drawn up in an arc from Habonville to Ste-Marie-aux-Chênes although still detached to IX Corps was 3 Guards Brigade of 2nd Guards Division at Habonville. Four Guards Brigade of 2nd Guards Division stood at St-Ail with 1st Guards Division at Ste-Marie-aux-Chênes. A mile behind Ste-Marie-aux-Chênes stood the ranks of X Corps although only its artillery was sent forward to support the forthcoming assault, the tactical conduct of which was to be in the hands of the Guards Commander, the 57-year-old Prince Augustus of Württemberg, a brave if unimaginative officer. His directions were for an assault in text-book order of solid half-battalion formations.

At just before 5 p.m. 3 Guards Brigade, consisting of the Guards Schützen Battalion and 1st and 3rd Guard Grenadier Regiments, Emperor Alexander's and Queen Elizabeth's, moved from their position on the right of 49 Hessian Brigade near Habonville. They were not to attack St-Privat but to pin down the right wing of IV Corps, General Cissey's Division, so as to prevent it intervening in the forthcoming main assault. Emerging from the Bois de la Cusse, they were met by the concentrated fire of IV Corps entrenched around Amanvillers. The assault was brought to a bloody halt on the open slope although the five battalions were able to deploy from column to line and hold a firing line in a more open formation. While the attention of Cissey's Division was now successfully held, it was at an appalling cost to 3 Guards Brigade who suffered some 2,440 killed and wounded within the space of forty minutes.

As the attack of 3 Guards Brigade developed,

at just after 5 p.m. the main assault on the St-Privat position began. Three brigades were to be involved and they were to attack from right to left, one after another.

First to go forward was 4 Guards Brigade of 2nd Guards Division, consisting of 2nd and 4th Guard Grenadier Regiments, Emperor Franz's and Queen Augusta's. They moved from just south of St-Ail, through the gun line, to form up for the assault just south of the Briey road. Still wearing their full marching packs and equipment weighing almost 100 pounds and formed in two ranks of half-battalions, they had more than one mile of open slope before them. Their objective was the

▲ *Even before the Guard began its fateful assault, its ranks had been thinned by artillery and long-range Chassepot fire. Someregiments spent up to an hour in this situation. (ASKB)*

▶ *When the order came to advance, the Guards moved off at the double with colours and field officers to the fore as if on the field of Waterloo. Their dense, half-battalion columns provided Canrobert's men with perfect targets as the Guards soon realized to their cost. (ASKB)*

◀ *Given the poor French deployment of the* mitrailleuse, *it is ironic that German tactics brought them into its effective range. Although its initial bursts could inflict massive casualties, the innate faults of this much vaunted weapon often left it jammed or with many barrels inoperative with broken firing pins. The bulk of German casualties were caused by the Chassepot and as a result of their own tactical formations. (ASKB)*

◀ *While the Guard fruitlessly assaulted St-Privat without artillery support, the Saxon artillery of XII Corps was brought to bear on Roncourt. This ensured its success without the scale of casualties suffered by the Guard. Once Roncourt had fallen the Saxon artillery was brought to bear on St-Privat. (ASKB)*

farm of Jerusalem just to the south of St-Privat which was held by General Lafont's Division. Advancing at the double with drums, flags and mounted officers to the front, the brigade's initial advance was most impressive. Having covered the first half of its course, at approximately 1,500 yards the Chassepots of Lafont's infantry, untouched at this stage by any supporting fire from the German guns, opened fire. It has been estimated that an average French division armed with Chassepots could deliver approximately 40,000 rounds per minute. Within a matter of minutes, both regiments were literally shot to pieces, losing most of their officers, 4th Guard all

their field officers. Two gun batteries moving up to give the brigade close fire support to the expected final assault were cut down before they could unlimber. By 5.20 the survivors were pinned down still some 800 yards from Lafont's men in a small depression across an otherwise smooth slope. The needle-guns' best range was little more than 700 yards and the few groups who tried to push on were cut down well before this.

Now, at 5.45, Prince Augustus ordered 1 Guards Brigade, commanded by General Kessel, consisting of 1st and 3rd Foot Guards Regiments, to advance. Their Divisional Commander, General

▶ *Rifleman, 1st Silesian Jäger Battalion, No. 5. The uniform of the Prussian Jäger distinguished them from the rest of the army. Apart from the traditional dark green coats and red facings, they wore conical shakos in place of the* **pickelhaube.** *While they still performed the function of skirmishers, their rifles were identical to those of the line regiments and as a result of the lessons of the war, their specialized role was to be merged with that of the regular infantry.*

Pape, had questioned this move as he had already watched the previous two assaults being slaughtered and was well aware that XI Corps was at least one hour away from any useful contribution. The Prince though was adamant and the Brigade moved up from its position just to the north of Ste-Marie-aux-Chênes. Having wheeled into two half-battalion lines just north of the Briey road, they advanced up the slope towards the Brigade of Tixier's Division which was waiting behind the thick stone walls of St-Privat itself, their left linked to Lafont's Division at Jerusalem. At 1,500 yards their majestic advance ended in the now familiar bloody heaps and by 6.15 its survivors were pinned down 700 yards from St-Privat's walls, the bodies of their dead comrades almost their only cover. According to the German account 'the slaughter was indescribable' as the Brigade's survivors stood amongst the bodies of more than 2,000 of its men.

Between the debris of 1 and 4 Guards Brigades was a gap traced by the Briey road itself which ran from Ste-Marie-aux-Chênes up to St-Privat. At just after 6.15 p.m. all but one battalion of 2 Guards Brigade, comprising 2nd and 4th Foot Guards Regiment, moved out of Ste-Marie-aux-Chênes astride the Briey road. Despite having already witnessed the slaughter of their predecessors, the guardsmen doubled into action and were likewise reduced to a bloody shambles at about 1,000 yards by the expected hail of bullets. A witness described them as 'moving forward as if in the teeth of a gale', but regardless of such determination they were halted broadly in line with the 1 and 4 Brigades' survivors.

By 6.30 p.m. the 18,000 men of 1st and 2nd Guards Divisions had suffered more than 8,000 casualties and the survivors had been reduced to a ragged skirmishing line. The loss of officers was especially severe, junior officers having to take command of battalions and NCOs companies. The battalion of the Guards Schützen, for example, had devolved upon a junior cadet. Yet all battalions continued to inch their way forward to within 600 yards of St-Privat and the flanking French positions around Jerusalem where they finally came to rest.

On the French side Canrobert could only be grateful for the mode of German attack, for his position was far more precarious than the previous hours' events would suggest. He was frankly amazed at the solid German infantry formations and the lack of artillery support for them, but he realized that this could not continue in so easy a fashion. Yet his repeated calls for reinforcements had only been answered with four additional artillery batteries and ammunition from the army reserve, the rest remaining six miles away at Plappeville. Bourbaki, whose untouched Guards Corps could have now decisively intervened at several points, imperiously ignored all calls for assistance, safe in the discretion Bazaine had granted him. On the French left, the German First Army was on the point of collapse, in the centre the XI Corps was exposed, and on the right the cream of the German Guard lay in bloody heaps. At any of these points Bourbaki's 20,000 men could have conceivably given France, the Second Empire and Bazaine a remarkable victory. Certainly at about 6.30 p.m. both Princes Augustus and Frederick Charles expected a French counter-attack to sweep the diminished ranks of the Guard off the slopes. Yet at that moment the force capable of this, Bourbaki's élite, sat listening to the sound of gunfire at Plappeville. When they did finally move a little while later the opportunity had passed.

Defeat

Just after 6.30 p.m. Frederick Charles ordered the action which ought to have preceded, not succeeded, the sacrifices of the Guard. The massed batteries of the Guard, XII and X Corps, some 208 guns, formed now in an arc through Ste-Marie-aux-Chênes, opened fire upon St-Privat. For more than forty minutes Canrobert's men in and around St-Privat were subjected to a tremendous bombardment. Having been unable to dig the trenches which Frossard's men had been able to do on the Point du Jour, the infantry of VI Corps were cruelly exposed on the ground. As the sun set, the flames and flying masonry of St-Privat and Jerusalem rose into the air. Canrobert knew that his men could not long survive this punishment, although few at this stage broke

under the hail of shells and detonations.

Now XII Corps finally produced the decisive moment. Since 5 p.m. under the command of the Crown Prince of Saxony, its leading elements had been attacking Roncourt to the north of St-Privat defended by Pechot's Brigade of five battalions and a single six-gun battery. For some two hours they had resisted, aware that they covered the flank of St-Privat. By 7 p.m., however, the full weight of XII Corps had finally driven Pechat's men out, although they fell back in good order to the Forest of Jaumount, thereby still covering VI Corps' escape route to Metz.

As XII Corps drove through Roncourt and on towards St-Privat at approximately 7.30, the survivors of the Guard rose and charged into the blazing ruins of St-Privat. The burning buildings now gave light to a vicious battle as the Guards and XII Corps fought to drive out its French defenders. Fifteen battalions of 45 and 47 Saxon Brigades now came in from the north and west sides of St-Privat supported by 84 Saxon guns at

▲ *By 7 p.m. the village of St-Privat was in flames and the ranks of VI Corps had been thinned by artillery fire. With the arrival of XII Corps from the north, the survivors of the* *Guard rose from their limited cover on the slope and drove into the remnans of Canrobert's men before the village walls. (ASKB)*

Roncourt. Fighting from house to house they drove into the centre of the village, the Guard intermingling with their ranks. Elements of the 4th Foot Guards Regiment stormed the cemetery while the fusilier battalion of 2nd Guard Grenadier Regiment took the farm buildings of Jerusalem. By 8 p.m. the defenders were broken and Canrobert's men poured back south-east as sheer weight of numbers finally told. On the German side exhaustion and confusion coupled with the d darkness inihibited any serious pursuit.

While the events at Roncourt had been developing and previous to this final assault, at just before 6.45 Bourbaki decided at last to bring

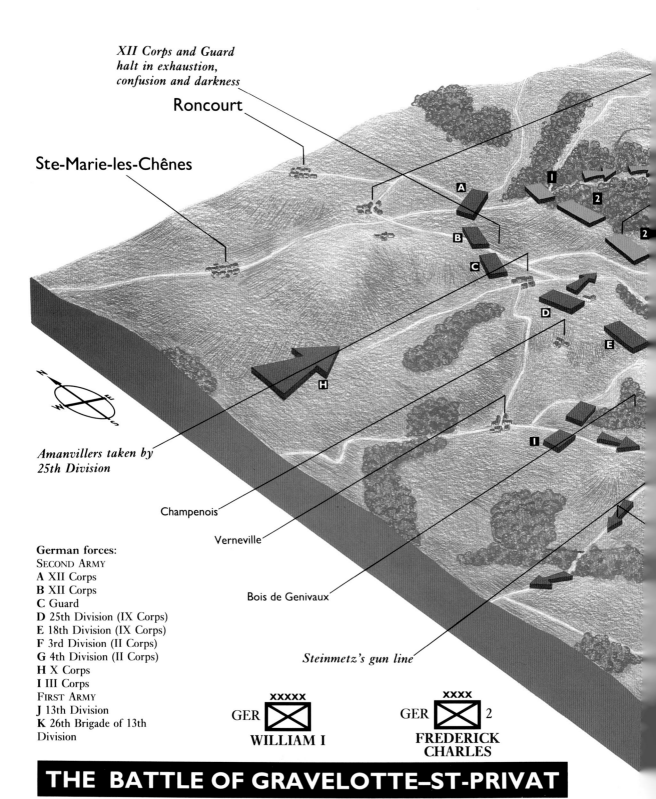

XII Corps and Guard halt in exhaustion, confusion and darkness

Roncourt

Ste-Marie-les-Chênes

Amanvillers taken by 25th Division

Champenois

Verneville

Bois de Genivaux

Steinmetz's gun line

German forces:
SECOND ARMY
A XII Corps
B XII Corps
C Guard
D 25th Division (IX Corps)
E 18th Division (IX Corps)
F 3rd Division (II Corps)
G 4th Division (II Corps)
H X Corps
I III Corps
FIRST ARMY
J 13th Division
K 26th Brigade of 13th Division

GER — **WILLIAM I**

GER — **FREDERICK CHARLES** 2

THE BATTLE OF GRAVELOTTE–ST-PRIVAT

8 p.m. 18 August 1870 – nightfall, and the collapse of the French right

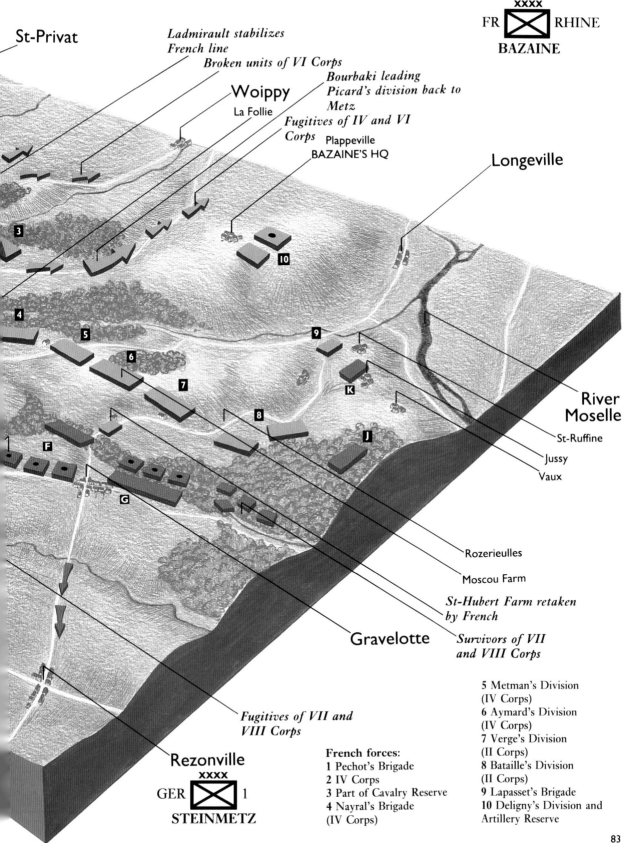

St-Privat

*Ladmirault stabilizes
French line*

Broken units of VI Corps

*Bourbaki leading
Picard's division back to
Metz*

Woippy

La Follie

*Fugitives of IV and VI
Corps* Plappeville

BAZAINE'S HQ

Longeville

FR XXXX RHINE

BAZAINE

3

4

5

6

7

8

F

G

9

K

J

River
Moselle

St-Ruffine

Jussy

Vaux

Rozerieulles

Moscou Farm

*St-Hubert Farm retaken
by French*

Gravelotte

*Survivors of VII
and VIII Corps*

*Fugitives of VII and
VIII Corps*

Rezonville

GER XXXX 1

STEINMETZ

French forces:
1 Pechot's Brigade
2 IV Corps
3 Part of Cavalry Reserve
4 Nayral's Brigade
(IV Corps)

5 Metman's Division
(IV Corps)
6 Aymard's Division
(IV Corps)
7 Verge's Division
(II Corps)
8 Bataille's Division
(II Corps)
9 Lapasset's Brigade
10 Deligny's Division and
Artillery Reserve

From north and west, the Guards and XII Corps fell upon the blazing ruins of St-Privat and its surrounding farmsteads. It is testament to both the Germans and French that the battle for the village was so intense; it was truly a contest of epic proportions. As night fell the weight of numbers drove the remains of VI Corps from the ruins of the village although neither the Guard nor XII Corps had the stamina to pursue them beyond. (ASKB)

With the collapse of
Canrobert's VI Corps,
not only those men but
fugitives from Ladmir-
ault's IV Corps and even
some of the cavalry
reserve joined the rout
back to Metz. Engulfing
Bourbaki's Guard, even
some of this élite lost
their nerve and joined the
throng. Despite this
panic, Ladmirault was
successful in
re-establishing a new
defensive line on the
ridge east of St-Privat
and Amanvillers from his
own largely intact corps,
the cavalry reserve and a
few surviving units of VI
Corps. (ASKB)

up his precious Guard to support Ladmirault and Canrobert. Either Ladmirault had launched a limited counter-attack to relieve the pressure on Canrobert had been met by the full weight of the Guard and IX Corps' artillery fire. Ladmirault and Canrobert had then been sending Bourbaki increasingly desperate requests for assistance as the German Guard and XII Corps' attacks developed. Bourbaki had finally decided to commit a division of his magnificent Guard, believing the situation offered an appropriate opportunity commensurate with the Guards' status, i.e., saving the situation from collapse. Yet as he emerged on to the plateau behind Ladmirault at the head of General Picard's Guard Grenadier Division, his columns were met by the first fugitives of VI Corps. As he pushed on, the crowds of fleeing soldiers became thicker and even his guardsmen became demoralized, a few even joining the fleeing soldiers. Bourbaki, primarily concerned and conscious of his own social status, turned to the officer from Ladmirault's staff sent to guide him up and stormed: 'You promised me victory, now you get me involved in a rout. You had no right to do that!' This prima donna of French generals turned his men around and headed them back to Plappeville. The sight of the Guard, its men obviously shaken, heading back in retreat was too much for the men of VI Corps and even some of IV Corps. Having been subjected to an intense bombardment since 6.30 p.m., and with their position collapsing, they broke and fled towards Metz.

At the same time Manstein's IX Corps pushed forward and stormed Amanvillers, his 25th Division moving a little way beyond. But Ladmirault was able to re-establish a line of sorts behind St-Privat and Amanvillers as darkness fell. The ground fell steeply east of St-Privat to the Bois de Jaumont where Pechot's Brigade had retired. Here also stood a brigade of Forton's cavalry division and a single regiment of *Chasseurs d'Afrique*. These linked with Ladmir-ault's men to create a stable line against the exhausted Guards and XII Corps who were satisfied to halt at St-Privat as night fell. Further, news of the collapse of First Army and uncertainty about the situation in the centre stilled any thoughts of launching into the darkness that lay behind St-Privat.

For the Germans it was not until past 11.30 that an overall picture began to emerge which indicated victory rather than defeat. At Imperial Headquarters, Moltke and the king believed that Steinmetz's rout indicated a draw at best if not a German defeat. It was only when news of the fall of St-Privat and the rout of VI Corps arrived that they realized they had successfully turned Bazaine's position and driven him back into the seige of Metz.

Bazaine had not had to wait so long to decide who had won for by 8 p.m. he was fully aware of the collapse of VI Corps. Already concerned at the high expenditure of ammunition and the apparent lack of reserves, other than in the magazines in Metz, these two factors provided him with the necessary excuse to continue his retreat to Metz. By 10 p.m. all French corps were preparing or had already begun to retreat the few remaining miles behind the line of forts around Metz.

Casualties

The broad totals are stark enough testament to the power of bolt-action rifles versus close-order frontal assault. The Germans lost 20,160 dead and wounded on the slopes of the French position against 7,855 French casualties plus 4,420 prisoners (half of whom were wounded), a total of 12,275. When broken down to localized comparisons the disparity is even greater. Frossard's II Corps lost 621 men while inflicting about 4,300 casualties on Steinmetz before the Point du Jour.

At individual unit level, the losses of the Guards before St-Privat are staggering. The battalion of the Guard Jäger lost nineteen officers, a surgeon and 431 men out of a morning total of some 700. The 2nd Foot Guards lost 39 officers and 1,076 men, the 3rd Foot Guards 36 officers and 1,060 men, almost half of their morning totals. On the French side, the units holding St-Privat each lost more than half their number in the village. While most Germans fell to Chassepot bullets, most French fell to Krupp shells. It is difficult to escape the conclusion that the heavy

▶ *Gunner, line artillery. Equipped with muzzle-loaded rifled guns, the French gunners were at a severe disadvantage against the breech-loaded Krupps, yet they were still able to inflict heavy casualties from their prepared positions. Apart from the change in cut, the distinction of the artillery uniforms had changed little since the First Empire, with short blue shell jackets faced red, as were the blue overalls. Armed with short carbines, some gunners had occasion to use these at Mars-la-Tour.*

▲ *As night fell, silence descended upon the battlefield. In the centre, before Amanvillers, the gunners of several Hessian batteries lay dead, having been within range of IV Corps' rifles all afternoon. Similar scenes were to be seen on the German right before St-Hubert and on the western edge of the Mance Ravine. The willingness of the German artillery to offer their infantry adequate close-fire support could not be better illustrated. (ASKB)*

German losses were avoidable given their artillery's unquestioned superiority. Finally, that the German artillery was willing to bring its guns forward to give valuable close fire support is illustrated by the four Hessian batteries east of Habonville. Despite losing seventeen officers, two surgeons, 187 men and 370 horses to Chassepot and case shot, they remained in action for more than three hours, only withdrawing from a lack of ammunition.

Judgement

The truth of the battle is that Bazaine had held the intention to retreat into Metz since the evening of the 16th and his mind was closed to all other possibilities. The various opportunities presented him throughout the long afternoon of the 18th to counter-attack were simply viewed by him as a successful defensive action prior to retreat. It seems fair to assume that Bazaine would have retreated once Canrobert was outflanked, whether or not First Army and the Guard had been driven off the field with an opportune counter-attack by Bourbaki's precious Guard supported by the Army's artillery reserve. Essentially Bazaine had been mentally defeated forty-eight hours earlier at Mars-la-Tour when the direct road to Verdun was cut. At his court-martial the reason he gave for retreating was that he had to replenish stocks of food and ammunition. This was completely untrue. The only factor lacking was the administrative competence to deliver the vast stocks available in Metz to the troops on the march. Proof that he always intended to continue his retreat on the 18th is demonstrated by his concern for his left flank, not his right, i.e. his line of retreat back into Metz.

Yet it should also be suggested that even had Bazaine seized the opportunity, it is questionable whether things would have been much different. If, for example, Bourbaki had committed himself on Ladmirault's front and a hole been punched in the German line at Vernéville, darkness would have limited any potential French advance. If the day had ended with Moltke retreating, he would still have been between Bazaine and Verdun and the German forces could afford the heavy casualties. As the subsequent weeks were to show, Moltke could afford to leave more than 200,000 men encircling Metz while continuing the campaign with another 200,000 troops. Essentially the superiority of the German military system came to the fore the longer the war lasted. Bazaine would have had to inflict three times the casualties on Moltke at each battle simply to maintain a position of numerical equality. Imperial France had few trained reserves to call upon, Germany had hundreds of thousands.

Having said this, Moltke cannot escape some censure for the events of the 18th. His original plan, though slightly flawed by a lack of reconnaissance, was essentially sound. that is, to pin the bulk of the French Army while enveloping it from the north, thereby also cutting its last line of possible retreat to Verdun. All Moltke had to do was to restrain his subordinates long enough to let it happen. This he failed to do with the result that the earlier lack of reconnaissance whereby he had underestimated the length of Bazaine's position now came into play. The enveloping movement took far longer and resulted in overstretching the German centre. This in itself was a serious flaw which was significantly compounded by Steinmetz and the Guards' suicidal assaults. Beyond sending a few written restraining orders, Moltke did little to intervene in the developing crisis. It might well be suggested that Moltke played the staff officer too much, failing to intervene in person when the occasion required. If the French had been commanded by an officer with any imagination or initiative, Moltke would have suffered a humiliating rebuff, if not outright defeat, on the actual field of battle. Moltke was fortunate in facing Bazaine: he did not have to pay the price of his failure to carry out adequate reconnaissance or to intervene in the afternoon's various sacrifices. Only his soldiers had to.

It is ironic that both Moltke and Bazaine spent much of the day as observers in the rear, doing little to intervene once the action began.

An analysis of the actual fighting shows that the soldiers of both sides fought well. The aggression of the German assaults was matched by the dogged defence of the French. Neither side had reason to feel ashamed of its soldiers' determination. The conclusion though as regards tactics was clear, the bolt-action rifle, the breech-loading artillery gun and the entrenching-tool made frontal assaults in close order a suicidal business. It was fortunate for the Germans that the French had only two of these three factors, while they held the other. Without the Krupps breech-loader, the outcome of the battle might have been very different. As it was the German infantry learnt quickly, if painfully, that an artillery bombardment followed by an advance in dispersed order was the only way forward. It is ironic that France's defeat in the war, due to poor leadership and an inadequate military system, obscured the potency of the defensive tactics its soldiers deployed.

The painful lessons that were demonstrated at Gravelotte–St-Privat would have be re-learnt forty-five years later in the trenches of the Western Front.

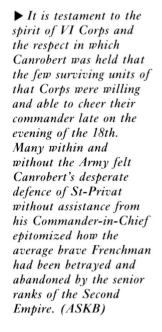

▶ *It is testament to the spirit of VI Corps and the respect in which Canrobert was held that the few surviving units of that Corps were willing and able to cheer their commander late on the evening of the 18th. Many within and without the Army felt Canrobert's desperate defence of St-Privat without assistance from his Commander-in-Chief epitomized how the average brave Frenchman had been betrayed and abandoned by the senior ranks of the Second Empire. (ASKB)*

AFTERMATH

While King William was sure that Gravelotte–St-Privat and the isolation of the Army of the Rhine marked the decisive point of the campaign, Moltke was not so sure. On the morning of 19 August he turned his mind westward to MacMahon at Châlons.

Having rested his men on the 19th and 20th, Moltke removed the Guard, IV and XII Corps from the Second Army of the Meuse and left its remaining four corps together with those of First Army under Frederick Charles to invest Metz. Third Army and the new Army of the Meuse under the Crown Prince of Saxony headed west on the 21st to close the campaign. Meanwhile Steinmetz was finally removed from doing any further mischief by being 'promoted' to Governor of Posen.

Meanwhile, on the French side Napoleon had been with MacMahon at Châlons since the 16th where a new army was being formed around the nucleus of I, V and VII Corps. With the new XII Corps of regulars under General Trochu, plus newly joined recruits and depot battalions to fill the gaps left by the frontier battles, and even eighteen battalions of the Guard Mobile of the Seine, an army of 130,000 men and 423 guns had been created by 21 August. In Paris, news of the early defeats and Bazaine's entrapment at Metz lead first to public gloom and then to fury. Repulican riots began and confidence in the Imperial regime plummeted. Consequently the Empress and Palikao bombarded the Emperor with messages insisting that he could not lead the Army of Châlons back to Paris as a defeated Emperor — the regime would collapse. With the public demanding that Bazaine be relieved, added to the need for 'victory', the subsequent course of events was dictated to MacMahon and Napoleon.

Accompanied by Napoleon, MacMahon's Army set out for Rheims and then Montmédy in an attempt to swing around Moltke's northern flank and relieve Metz. If such a move could have been successful, it would have also placed the French across the German lines of communication, with a heavily fortified Paris to the west. Yet by the 24th Moltke was fully aware of MacMahon's movements and he quickly seized the opportunity to encircle and destroy him.

The numerically and morally superior German forces swung north-west and on the 30th the cavalry patrols of Third Army found MacMahon fifteen miles south-east of Sedan at Beaumont-sur-Meuse where a small action ensued. With part of his army beaten at Beaumont on the 30th, MacMahon fell back to Sedan to regroup, not realizing that he was falling into a trap. On 1 September, with some 100,000 demoralized men and supplies for only a few days, MacMahon found himself encircled on 1 September by some 200,000 men. The Battle of Sedan was a foregone conclusion, desperation and honour being the motivating factor on the French side.

As MacMahon and the Emperor surrendered with the last army of the Second Empire, the campaign begun only four weeks earlier ended. The Empire itself collapsed on 4 September and the newly proclaimed Republic then endured the Siege of Paris and the desperate campaigns of the autumn and winter. On 28 October Bazaine had finally surrendered the entire Army of the Rhine at Metz, the last outpost of the Empire.

While France underwent political revolution and military defeat, Germany became an Empire on 18 January 1871 in the reflected glory of victory. The war itself ended on 23 January as France accepted defeat and humiliation.

THE BATTLEFIELD TODAY

The battlefield of Gravelotte–St-Privat is remarkably little changed from the way it was on 18 August 1870. Apart from numerous memorials and improved roads, the woods, fields and villages are much as they were.

The City of Metz has not expanded sufficiently on the south-west bank of the Moselle to impinge on the area of actual fighting and the various villages and farms leave one with the feeling that they look now much as they did on the morning of the 18th. The Forts of St-Quentin and Plappeville still stand, as do most of the forts around the city, although they are now on the edge of the modern suburbs rather than in green fields as in 1870. At the southern end of the battlefield the Mance stream still runs down the flat floor of the ravine, its steep slopes still covered in dense undergrowth and trees. Above it the various farms and buildings of Leipzig, Moscow, St-Hubert and the Point du Jour still gaze down from the ridge.

Moving north, the gentler open slopes around the village of Amanvillers help convey the isolation of Manstein as he struck towards the French centre. Amanvillers itself is still a tiny one-street village with nothing to indicate that it was once the centre of a ferocious battle.

Finally one comes to St-Privat, sitting atop the slopes gently rolling away to the west. Although completely rebuilt after the battle, the village does not appear to have expanded much, if at all, and the rebuilding was very much in the previous style. What is most striking is to gaze down towards Ste-Marie-aux-Chênes and St-Ail across the still bare slopes to realize the utter lack of cover. The village of Roncourt to the north and the tiny farm of Jerusalem just to the south also appear unchanged. Looking south-west from St-Privat, the rolling countryside across which Moltke's men advanced stretches out to Vionville and Rezonville, a view enjoyed from most of the French positions.

As for battlefield monuments, the majority are to the German regiments. On the bare slopes below St-Privat four or five dot the landscape such as those to the Emperor Alexander's and Queen Elizabeth's Regiments, seemingly marking the line where the Guard was brought to a halt. To the south, in the Mance Ravine there are a number to regiments of Steinmetz's ill-used army, one of the most impressive being to the 8th Jäger Battalion at the edge of the road between Gravelotte and St-Hubert. The fields and woods around St-Hubert are dotted with memorials, testaments to the desperate attempts to seize and hold a lodgement there. The only obvious French monument is at St-Privat where Canrobert's men are remembered for their part in the epic contest with the German Guard and Saxons.

CHRONOLOGY

1857 Helmuth von Moltke becomes Chief of the Prussian General Staff.

1862 Albert von Roon commences reforms of Prussian Army.

Sept Count Otto von Bismarck appoointed Chief Minister of Prussia.

1864 Second Schleswig-Holstein War. Feb-Apr Austro-Prussian Army defeats Danes.
1866

June–July Austro-Prussian War.

3 July Battle of Sadowa (Königgrätz)

23 Aug Treaty of Prague excludes Austria from Germany.

1867 North German Confederation creates a united Germany north of the River Main.

20 Jan Marshal Neil replaces Randon as Minister of War and begins army reforms including introduction of Chassepot rifle.

26 July Secret clause negotiated at Nikolsburg sees southern German states agree to reorganize armies on Prussian model and join with the Confederation in case of war.

Sept 1868 Military coup in Spain deposes Queen Isabella II.

Sept 1869 The Spanish make first approach to Prince Charles Anton of Hohenzollern-Sigmaringen.

1870

8 July Benedetti dispatched to Ems to demand candidature be withdrawn.

13 July Bismarck re-structures the Ems Telegram so as to suggest demand for withdrawal of candidature rejected outright.

19 July French declaration of war received in Berlin.

2 Aug Campaign opens with the Army of the Rhine advancing to seize Saarbrücken.

4 Aug Moltke launches German offensive with the advance of Third Army against Wissembourg.

5 Aug Steinmetz unilaterally assumes offensive with First Army.

6 Aug Battles of Fröschwiller-Wörth and Spicheren.

7 Aug Napoleon orders retreat on Châlons via Metz.

8 Aug Bazaine receives command of II, III and IV Corps.

10 Aug Moltke issues orders to concentrate German armies towards Metz and the encirclement of the Army of the Rhine.

12 Aug Bazaine receives command of the Army of the Rhine although Napoleon does not depart for Châlons until morning of 16th.

16 Aug Battle of Mars-la-Tour.

17 Aug The Army of the Rhine occupies the Amanvillers ridge.

18 Aug Battle of Gravelotte St-Privat.

8 a.m. Moltke orders advance.

12 p.m. Manstein opens battle before Amanvillers with artillery of 25th Infantry Division.

2.30 p.m. Steinmetz unilaterally launches VIII Corps across Mance Ravine.

3 p.m. Massed guns of VII and VIII Corps open fire in support of attack across Mance Ravine.

4 p.m. Steinmetz orders VII Corps forward, followed by Ist Cavalry Division.

4.50 p.m. 3 Guards Brigade opens attack on Canrobert's position at St-Privat.

5.15 p.m. 4 Guards Brigade advances against Canrobert's position.

5.45 p.m. 1 Guards Brigade advances against Canrobert's position.

6.15 p.m. 2 Guards Brigade advances against Canrobert's position. Steinmetz commits last reserves of First Army across the Mance Ravine.

6.30 p.m. A considerable proportion of VII and VIII Corps disintegrate and flee back towards Rezonville. Frederick Charles orders massed guns to destroy Canrobert's position.

7 p.m. 3rd Division of Fransecky's II Corps advances across Ravine. XII Corps clears Roncourt and with survivors of the Guard attacks ruins of St-Privat.

8 p.m. Arrival of 4th Division of II Corps. German right on Mance Ravine stabilized. St-Privat falls and Canrobert's Corps largely collapses. Bourbaki refuses to commit Guard to this 'defeat'!

10 p.m. Firing largely dies down across battlefield.

19 Aug The Army of the Rhine retreats into Metz.

21 Aug Moltke resumes advance, his objective MacMahon's Army of Châlons.

1 Sept Battle of Sedan. The Army of Châlons encircled and surrenders with Napoleon.

4 Sept The Second Empire is declared at an end and is replaced by a Government of National Defence.

A GUIDE TO FURTHER READING

ADRIANCE, T.J. *The Last Gaiter Button*, Connecticut, 1987. An excellent study of the deficiencies of French mobilization in 1870.

The War Diary of the Emperor Frederick III 1870-71 (translated and edited by A.R. Allinson), London, 1927. A day by day record of the armies' movements.

ASCOLI, D. *A Day of Battle*, London, 1987. Unquestionably the best and most accessible account of the campaign up to Sedan, although the main focus is the Battle of Mars-la-Tour.

The Franco-German War of 1870-71, German General Staff (translated by Captain F.C.H Clarke), 5 vols, London 1874-84. While the most detailed account available, it is, for obvious reasons, weighted on the German side.

CREVELD, M. van. *Supplying War: Logistics from Wallenstein to Patton*, Cambridge, 1977. This has a valuable chapter on the problems both sides had with logistics and its impact on the campaign.

GOLITZ, W. *The German General Staff*, London, 1953. A comprehensive and balanced analysis of the role, strengths and weaknesses of this key institution.

HOLMES, R. *The Road to Sedan*, London, 1984. A fine and detailed study of the French Army in the decades prior to 1870, highlighting its strengths and fundamental weaknesses.

HOWARD, M. *The Franco-Prussian War*, London, 1961. Still the finest overall account of the entire war.

THOMPSON, J.M. *Louis Napoleon and the Second Empire*, Oxford, 1954. A comprehensive and balanced account of this eventually tragic figure and the causes of his downfall.

WARGAMING
GRAVELOTTE–ST-PRIVAT

From a wargaming point of view, the Franco-Prussian War has a good deal to recommend it. In common with the earlier wars of Marlborough, Frederick and Napoleon, the uniforms have considerable visual appeal, those of the French army being particularly elegant. Tactically the contest between the greatly superior French rifle and more efficient German guns provides a challenging problem for both sides. The French, able to punish the German infantry at ranges that preclude an effective reply, are themselves inadequately protected by their own inferior guns from the accurate and destructive Krupps. Strategically the widespread use of railways, not just for the initial concentration on the frontier, but also for the movement of troops and supplies within the theatre of operations, opens up interesting possibilities for a wargames campaign. So too does the extensive use made of the telegraph, which greatly speeds up communications – although both are vulnerable to enemy action.

From the gaming point of view, the different facets of the war can be approached in different ways. In the realms of strategy, a map campaign, conducted without figures, but with an active umpire, can offer a good insight into the problems encountered by the real-life commanders. One example of this would be a game designed to simulate the mobilization and concentration of the armies from their homes and depots to the frontier. For the Germans this would involve the calling out of their reservists, embodying them into the existing regiments and their transportation to the concentration areas. The detailed staff work involved might be made the subject of a committee game, with the Chief-of-Staff (Moltke) overseeing the whole operation, with subordinates dealing with the call-up, supply, transportation, railway time-tables and so on. The umpire would keep the players informed of progress and of any problems arising through the 'friction of war'. These difficulties might include, for example, a serious traffic jam at a rail junction or the loss of a vital bridge.

A similar exercise involving the French would need to reflect the difficulties caused by their less efficient military system. Reservists recalled to the colours would first need to travel to their respective regimental depots to receive their equipment. This could involve a journey of perhaps many hundreds of miles. Once this were completed, the men would then have to find their regiments, who could already be on the move from their garrison areas. The likely result is that many units will be either under-strength or slow in reaching their concentration areas. The lack of central direction in the control of railway movement would also have to be reflected by the umpire, traffic jams and the consequent delays posing a serious problem. The collection, movement and distribution of supplies by the over-centralized *Intendance* also had an unfortunate effect on the French troops, many of whom were short not only of food but of quite basic items of equipment, such as tents and cooking utensils. Through such an exercise it can be appreciated that an army could be seriously weakened both in body and in spirit before a shot was fired.

A logistics game such as this might be carried out either as an end in itself, or as a preliminary to a more orthodox campaign. In the latter case, the success with which each side is able to summon, equip and concentrate its forces would have a direct bearing on the way the campaign itself is conducted. The French, for example, had intended (and the Germans certainly expected) that they would be able to take advantage of the fact that a higher proportion of their troops were long-service regulars, and launch a pre-emptive strike into German territory, in the hope of disrupting enemy mobilization. The farcical chaos of their own mobilization made this impossible. As a result France rather than Germany was invaded.

An alternative to refighting the whole war – a very time-consuming undertaking – would be to concentrate on one particular part of it, such as the battle for the frontier or the Sedan or Metz campaigns. Each could be firmly set in its historical context with the troops available at the time. The latter of the three, for example, might deal with the hand-over of command from Napoleon to Bazaine on the 12th and the subsequent attempt to withdraw on Châlons-sur-Marne. This would work particularly well as a committee game, with players representing all the senior commanders, including those of the artillery, engineers and supply services, as well as the Cassandra-like figure of the Emperor himself. The objective would be to withdraw the army over the River Moselle, move it over the difficult terrain to the Gravelotte plateau, and thence down the road to Verdun, before it can be cut off by the advancing Germans. Each of the players would be concerned with matters affecting their own branch of the service; for example, General Soleille, commanding the artillery, would have as his objective the husbanding of the ammunition – it was he who, after Mars-la-Tour, misled Bazaine regarding the amounts available. The role of the umpire would be to issue reports to the players regarding such things as sightings of the enemy, the movement of their own troops and convoys and the state of the roads and weather. Failure to work out sensible orders of march or to send out reconnaissance patrols would be severely punished. Such a 'paper' exercise, while perhaps lacking the glamour and excitement of more conventional wargaming, would certainly require more thought, planning and cooperation, and engender greater empathy with the real-life commanders.

Moving on to the more traditional table-top encounters at the tactical and grand tactical level, we are faced with the question: what characterized the battles of the Franco-Prussian war? While wargaming is inevitably, and thankfully, a pale imitation of the real thing, any set of rules must at least make an effort to reflect these perceived realities. As regards doctrine, the French commanders were seemingly obsessed by the idea of defending strong positions and inviting the enemy to destroy himself upon them. Ironically, the Germans seemed only too happy to oblige, Steinmetz's sacrifice of First Army at Gravelotte being the obvious example. They did, however, appreciate the value of outflanking moves and used them to great effect at Spircheren, Froeschwiller and St-Privat, although on each occasion only following a costly and unsuccessful frontal assault.

Surprisingly, the French were particularly conservative in their use of artillery (Napoleon's favourite arm), often keeping their corps and army batteries in reserve for a decisive intervention that never came. The Germans, on the other hand, repeatedly pushed their guns into the thick of the fighting, often without infantry support; Manstein's use (or misuse) of his guns in front of Amanvillers is a case in point. This could easily be reflected in a game by requiring each French corps commander to throw a die to 'release' his reserve artillery, whilst the Germans would have most if not all of their guns available at the start. The idiosyncracies of the French fuzes should also be allowed for, with enhanced fire bonuses within their restricted bursting bands. The mis-applied, though undoubtedly effective, mitrailleuses should also be considered. Under the right conditions they proved to be deadly but could not defend themselves against the German guns.

The battlefield role of cavalry had also been transformed by 1870, although many commanders had obviously failed to appreciate this. Against formed troops, a frontal attack was invariably suicidal, although the German cavalry at Mars-la-Tour did perform useful service, particularly von Bredow's men.

As with any re-fight of an historical battle, the problem of hindsight remains the most intractable. This battle, in common with many others throughout history, was a catalogue of errors and misjudgements, which players are unlikely to repeat unless obliged to do so. Going through the sequential events of the real battle, though instructive on an historical level, would provide a rather sterile game, particularly for the Germans, who were severely beaten at almost every point. After all, how many wargamers would willingly emulate the débâcle in the Mance ravine, Manstein's reckless squandering of his guns or the sacrifice of the Guard at St-Privat?

What choices then are left? One option would be to have a player representing Moltke, as Commander-in-Chief, while the other players command the various divisions. During the battle the divisional commanders were not able to display the same level of initiative that they had in earlier encounters, largely due to the fact that Gravelotte-St-Privat was the first set-piece battle of the war, deliberately brought on by both Moltke and Bazaine, rather than one of dispersed forces marching to the sound of the guns. Consequently the plan of action was more carefully considered (although not always so carefully carried out), with less room for individual initiative on the part of the more junior officers. The umpire could then assume the role of the army and corps commanders, receiving instructions from above, interpreting, misinterpreting or simply ignoring them before issuing orders to the divisions. In this way the crisis of command in the German armies on the day (it was scarcely less than this), could be repeated, as almost all the errors were committed at the army and corps level.

For the French the situation is a little different. For them it was the Commander-in-Chief who proved to be the real liability. The various corps, once deployed, changed their stance but little throughout the day. Indeed it was scarcely necessary for them to do so as they defended their positions with relative ease and did not feel inclined to launch unauthorized counter-attacks. Only at St-Privat was there any real manoeuvring, and it was here that the battle was lost. Consequently, for the French the umpire could take on the role of Bazaine, with players taking command of the various corps. They would only be able to communicate with the C-in-C or each other through written messages. In this way the umpire would be well placed to frustrate the French players, particularly Canrobert, by his inaction, perhaps sending the odd wagon-load of ammunition or *Légion d'honneur*, but providing no overall leadership.

With the umpire's adoption of this somewhat schizophrenic role of French C-in-C and German army/corps commanders, something like a realistic atmosphere could be achieved. It would, one hopes, result in frustrated and isolated French corps commanders in good defensive positions but with little assistance from (or faith in) their chief, coming under repeated but disjointed assaults from German divisional commanders sent on madcap errands by their foolhardy superiors, while Moltke looks on in horror. By removing the mainspring of decision-making from the players, they would have little option but to concentrate on handling the troops under their immediate command and trusting to providence. It would probably be preferable to have the action taking place on a number of separate tables, so that the isolation of the players is increased. In fact, the battle does divide quite conveniently, with First Army facing the French II and III Corps, Manstein the IV Corps and the Guard and the Saxons confronting Canrobert. This would obviously make any inter-player cooperation much more difficult.

Another option would be to fight a part of the battle at a different level of command. 'The Defence of St.-Privat' could be made into an interesting theme, with players taking on the role of Canrobert and his divisional commanders, with perhaps a chief of staff and artillery commander. The latter would have the difficult job of husbanding VI Corps' limited artillery resources. The German players would represent the commander of Second Army, those of the Guard and Saxon Corps, and their respective divisional and artillery chiefs. The game would hinge around the successful coordination of the Guard advance through Ste.-Marie and the Saxon turning movement via Roncourt. There should be a strong possibility – the umpire comes in again here – of either Frederick Charles or Augustus of Württemberg losing patience and attacking before the Saxons are in position. The defence of Roncourt would therefore take on great significance in this regard: any time the French could gain here would delay the Saxon advance and perhaps precipitate a premature attack on the part of the Guard. Again it needs to be emphasized that the role of the umpire is vital as he is able to introduce the element of chance that no set of rules, however comprehensive, can hope to include.